Bright Young Things

Bright Young Things

LIFE IN THE
ROARING TWENTIES

ALISON MALONEY

Bespoke illustrations by
Katie May

Virgin BOOKS

2 4 6 8 10 9 7 5 3 1

First published in 2012 by Virgin Books, an imprint of Ebury Publishing

A Random House Group Company

www.randomhouse.co.uk

Addresses for companies within The Random House Group Limited can be found at www.randomhouse.co.uk/offices.htm

The Random House Group Limited Reg. No. 954009

A CIP catalogue record for this book is available from the British Library

The Random House Group Limited supports The Forest Stewardship Council (FSC®), the leading international forest certification organisation. Our books carrying the FSC label are printed on FSC® certified paper. FSC is the only forest certification scheme endorsed by the leading environmental organisations, including Greenpeace. Our paper procurement policy can be found at www.randomhouse.co.uk/environment

MIX
Paper from
responsible sources
FSC® C016897

Designed by K DESIGN, Winscombe, Somerset
Printed and bound by CPI Group (UK) Ltd, Croydon, CR0 4YY

ISBN: 9780753540978

To buy books by your favourite authors and register for offers, visit www.randomhouse.co.uk

CONTENTS

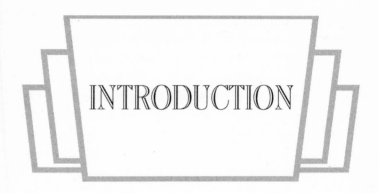

INTRODUCTION

' *The parties were bigger. The pace was
faster, the shows were broader, the
buildings were higher, the morals were
looser, and the liquor was cheaper.* '

F Scott Fitzgerald on the 1920s in *The Great Gatsby*

Coming hard on the heels of the First World War, the 1920s ushered in a decadent decade of celebration for the young, the rich and the talented. It was the jazz age: a time for cocktails, illegal nightclubs and outrageous fancy dress parties. It was the era of the flapper, when liberated girls cut their hair, shortened their skirts and started smoking and drinking. It was the time of the Charleston, when debutantes and princes shared dance floors with gangsters and drug dealers ... and everyone danced all night.

With the war consigned to history – and the decline of the aristocracy as yet a distant threat – the twenties were a golden age. The previous decade had been dominated by war, with men from all walks of life fighting and dying on the battlefields of Europe, while women filled the shoes of their absent menfolk in the workplace and gained a newfound independence as a result. As the 1920s dawned, a new generation who had lost older brothers and fathers, but who had escaped the conflict themselves, were becoming adults. The shackles of wartime gave way to the euphoria of peacetime freedom and the sadness of loss made the young survivors all the more determined to live life to the full.

The rich, young and beautiful of elite London society – the Mayfair set in particular – blasted into the Roaring Twenties in a cacophony of motorcars, loud parties and shocking antics. Dubbed the 'Bright Young People' by the British press, they made headlines and filled endless gossip columns with their scandalous costume parties, bathing parties and midnight scavenger hunts.

In the United States, meanwhile, Prohibition sparked the rise of speakeasies and Mafia mobs, and Wall Street merrily traded with no hint of the impending crash of '29. In Paris, novelists and artists hung out with exotic dancers in seamy nightclubs, forming a new avant-garde.

As the novelist Barbara Cartland explained in her autobiography, *We Danced All Night*: 'We were like nuns who had never seen over the convent wall until now. Everything was unexpected, fascinating, thrilling, unusual.'

The twenties, perhaps more than any other decade, expressed an explosion of *joie de vivre* for a post-war generation for whom life was to be lived with no-holds-barred passion. It was party time at last ...

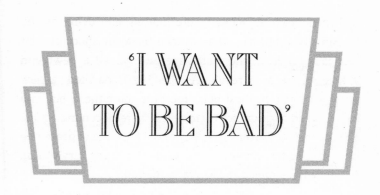

'I WANT TO BE BAD'

If it's naughty to rouge your lips,
Shake your shoulders and shake your hips,
Then the answer is, "I wanna be bad!"

Ray Henderson, Lew Brown,
Buddy DeSylva, 'I Want to Be Bad'

The twenties were the years of the bob-haired, calf-flashing flapper, who stayed out late and danced the Charleston. But being a flapper was more than a fashion statement; it was an attitude. The headstrong, carefree and liberated young women of the era attended jazz clubs and parties, drove cars, drank alcohol and smoked – always with a long cigarette holder, naturally. They used modern slang, calling things 'the bee's knees' and 'the cat's pyjamas', and were thought to have loose sexual morals.

Although many were wealthy, these impetuous creatures were often scorned by their aristocratic peers as 'nouveau riche'. Loelia Ponsonby, later the Duchess of Westminster, was a young debutante in the early 1920s. In her autobiography *Grace and Favour*, she remembered, 'Teenagers had not been invented. I doubt my parents knew what an adolescent was. Flappers were definitely middle class.'

A Testament to Youth

In 1923 journalist Samuel Hopkins Adams published the novel *Flaming Youth* under the pseudonym Warner Fabian. The heroine, Patricia Frentiss, is the archetypal flapper and the author's dedication summed up the wild young women of the Roaring Twenties:

To the woman of the period thus set forth, restless, seductive, greedy, discontented, craving sensation, unrestrained, a little morbid, more than a little selfish, slack of mind as she is trim of body, neurotic and vigorous, a worshipper of tinsel gods at perfumed altars, fit mate for the hurried, reckless and cynical man of the age, predestined mother of – what manner of being? To her I dedicate this study of herself.

Defining the Flapper

The word 'flapper' originally meant a very young girl, likened to a young bird that is learning to fly.

In northern slang, a flapper was a girl with flapping pigtail, illustrated by a 1910 article in *The Times*, which stated, 'A "flapper", we may explain, is a young lady who has not yet been promoted to long frocks and the wearing of her hair "up".'

However 'flap' was also an ancient term for prostitute and by the end of the First World War, the flapper had grown up from a mischievous teenager to the brazen young woman we now know.

In a 1920 lecture, Dr R Murray-Leslie claimed the lack of eligible young men in post-war Britain had created 'the social butterfly type; the frivolous, scantily clad, jazzing flapper, irresponsible and undisciplined, to whom a dance, a new hat, or a man with a car, were of more importance than the fate of nations.'

Going Up in Smoke

Drinking and smoking in public became a symbol of female emancipation seized on by the eager flapper. In previous years it was considered unbecoming of the fairer sex to touch alcohol outside of private homes and social events, but the rise of the nightclub and, in the US, the speakeasy changed that.

Similarly, smoking in public had been a taboo for women until the twenties. In the US, a female smoker could be arrested in the early 1900s and it wasn't until 1929 that a ban on women lighting up in railway carriages was lifted. Cigarette manufacturers soon

got wise to the new market, and US favourite Lucky Strike used pictures of attractive young ladies enjoying the 'Torches of Liberty' at suffragette marches in New York.

The brand also promoted the cigarette as a slimming aid, using actress Constance Talmadge, an actress and famous flapper, in a 1927 ad which urged girls to 'Reach for a Lucky instead of a sweet.'

Speak Easy

'Now I am old-fashioned. A woman, I consider, should be womanly. I have no patience with the modern neurotic girl who jazzes from morning to night, smokes like a chimney, and uses language which would make a Billingsgate fishwoman blush!'

From *Murder on the Links* by Agatha Christie

Who's That Girl? Zelda Fitzgerald

— ★ —

Famous For: After filling the gossip columns in Alabama, she married author F Scott Fitzgerald in 1920 and the couple became the darlings of the New York literary set, drinking with Ernest Hemingway and Dorothy Parker.

— ★ —

Career Notes: Dubbed 'The First American Flapper' by her husband, she became the model for the heroines in his bestselling novels, including *The Beautiful and the Damned* and *Tender is the Night*. Diagnosed with schizophrenia in 1930, she spent much of her later life in asylums, dying in a hospital fire in 1948, eight years after Fitzgerald.

— ★ —

Sound Bite: In the article 'Eulogy on the Flapper', published in *Metropolitan* magazine, Zelda wrote, 'Mothers disapproved of their sons taking the Flapper to dances, to teas, to swim and most of all to heart.'

Famous Flappers

Clara Bow, Louise Brooks and Joan Crawford all epitomised the flapper on the silver screen but perhaps the most iconic of them all, in looks and lifestyle, was the hedonistic Zelda Fitzgerald. Claiming she was no good at anything but 'useless pleasure-giving pursuits', she lived for the party lifestyle and drove her husband, F Scott Fitzgerald, crazy by stripping off at parties and flirting with his closest friends.

Chop Chop!

Columnist Louella Parsons interviewed the eighteen-year-old actress Clara Bow for the *New York Telegraph* in July 1922 and described her as 'the flapper who now flaps in up-to-date juvenile society. She is the unconscious flapper.'

Asked whether she wanted to eat lunch at 'the Astor, the Biltmore or the Chatham?' she gave the archetypal 'flapper' response. 'Let's go to a chop suey place,' said Clara. 'I know a wonderful restaurant here on Broadway where they dance at noon – don't you love to dance?'

The song 'Tea for Two' from the 1930 musical *No, No, Nanette* has the 'Flippant young flappers' singing of 'Petting parties with the smarties. Dizzy with dangerous glee.'

Petting Parties

The original flappers hailed from the jazz clubs of the United States and brought with them a more liberated view of sex. The 'petting party', where teenagers kissed and cuddled to their heart's content, was born and spread like wildfire among the young socialites of the American scene.

In his first novel, *This Side of Paradise*, F Scott Fitzgerald wrote, 'On the Triangle trip Amory had come into constant contact with that great current American phenomenon, the "petting party". None of the Victorian mothers – and most of the mothers were Victorian – had any idea how casually their daughters were accustomed to be kissed. "Servant-girls are that way," said Mrs. Houston-Carmelite to her popular daughter. "They are kissed first and proposed to afterward."'

For most young women, however, the petting was reasonably innocent and, if it went further than a kiss, was usually within a long-term relationship or perhaps engagement.

An 'Anti-petting League' set up by female students at the University of Southern California decreed that a girl should only have sexual contact with a man she intended to marry. The rule stated: 'She must kiss and squeeze and be kissed and squeezed by only a man to whom she is engaged.'

Speak Easy

'"I do not want to be respectable because respectable girls are not attractive" ... "boys do dance most with the girls they kiss most" ...

'Perceiving these things, the Flapper awoke from her lethargy of sub-deb-ism, bobbed her hair, put on her choicest pair of earrings and a great deal of audacity and rouge and went into the battle. She flirted because it was fun to flirt.'

From 'Eulogy on the Flapper' by Zelda Fitzgerald,
published in *Metropolitan* magazine, 1922

Scourge of Society

The precocious, carefree, modern girl was frowned upon by society and frequently berated in conservative newspapers such as the *Daily Mail*. Eminent doctor and sociologist Arabella Kenealy, writing in 1920, claimed, 'Many of our young women have become desexed and masculinised, with short hair, skirts no longer than kilts, narrow hips, insignificant breasts.' But she could also see the positives, going on to say, 'There has arrived a confident, active, game-loving, capable human being who shuns the servitude of household occupations.'

In Defence of a Flapper

Other scholars and medics were also excited about women's changing identities. In his 1924 lecture on psychoanalysis, eminent psychologist Dr Frank Stanton claimed the flapper was a more honest creature than her mother and one with more common sense. In an article in the Connecticut paper the *Hartford Daily Courant*, he is reported to have said:

> *People have been afraid of admitting their natural longings and have become unhappy and ingrown. The Flapper knows what she wants and goes after it. Her cigarettes and snappy manner are her first feeble symptoms of her declaration of independence. She is fast becoming rationalised as she understands herself better. She is the hope of the future and we should be proud of her.*

Poetic Licence

In 1922, reader Laurena Berg sent a poem called 'Version of a Flapper' to the *Los Angeles Times*. The four stanzas, published as a letter under the heading, 'The Flapper Flaps', are preceded by the words, 'I am a Flapper and in self-defence I wrote this verse.' Laurena's poem sums up the rebellious nature of this new breed, ending with:

> *If she likes a lot of boys,*
> *She's a Flapper*
> *If she uses hearts for toys,*
> *She's a Flapper.*
> *If she's really wide awake*
> *If she's game to give and take,*
> *If she lives for pleasure's sake,*
> *She's a Flapper.*

Speak Easy

'[Flappers] were smart and sophisticated, with an air of independence about them ... I don't know if I realised as soon as I began seeing them that they represented the wave of the future, but I do know I was drawn to them. I shared their restlessness, understood their determination to free themselves of the Victorian shackles of the pre-World War One era and find out for themselves what life was all about.'

Silent film actress Colleen Moore
in her autobiography *Silent Star*

Smart Talk

The true flapper shot from the lip, with slang phrases designed to show how hip and modern she was. Here are a few of the popular slang terms of the 1920s:

Alarm clock – chaperone

Alibi – bunch of flowers

Appleknocker – a yokel or hick

Applesauce – flattery or flannel

Barney-mugging – love-making

Biscuit – a pettable girl

Butt me – give me a cigarette

Cake basket – Limousine

Clothes line – a neighbourhood gossip

Corn-shredder – young man who treads on one's feet when dancing

Dapper – father

> *Terms for things that are good:*
> The cat's pyjamas, the bee's knees, the elephant's instep, ritzy, spiffy, swanky, swell, ducky, hotsy-totsy, It.
> *Terms for things that are bad:*
> Banana oil, bunk, hokum, hooey, horse feathers, lousy.

Dimbox – taxi
Dingledangler – a persistent caller on the phone
Dropping the pilot – getting divorced
Finale hopper – a man who arrives after the bill is paid
Flat tire – dull person
Handcuff – engagement ring
Hush money – allowance from parents
Let's blouse – let's go
Oilcan – imposter
Plastered – drunk
Snugglepups – young men at petting parties
Sugar – money
Whisk broom – man with facial hair

Hopping the Pond

The cult of the flapper originated in the United States, but by the dawn of the decade, her carefree attitude and party lifestyle had already spread through the drawing rooms of London and infected the wealthy young aesthetes of Chelsea and Mayfair. In post-war Britain, the era of the Bright Young People was born.

BRIGHT YOUNG PEOPLE

Bright Young People,
Ready to do and to dare,
We casually strive, to keep London alive,
From Chelsea to Bloomsbury Square.

Noël Coward, 'Bright Young People'

Outrageous antics, all-night parties and high-speed treasure hunts filled the fun-packed days of the Bright Young People. For this small group of artists, writers and socialites, London in the 1920s was a playground of hedonism and thrill-seeking. Their festivities filled the daily gossip pages in the tabloid press, who gave them their famous nickname, while their elders tutted over their wild behaviour and uncaring attitude.

While newspapers and advertisers tried to capture the zeitgeist of the wider group of the 'Bright Young Things', meaning anyone between eighteen and thirty-five, the Bright Young People were a much more select band – legends of the London social scene.

The Mayfair Set

But who were these lucky Bohemians whose only ambition was making whoopee?

Not all the Bright Young People came from rich aristocratic families and upper-class circles. Many came from the 'nouveau riche' set, whose parents had amassed wealth through business or commerce, while others, like Evelyn Waugh and Cecil Beaton, came from modest homes and found themselves mixing with the 'smart set' in the drinking dens of Mayfair by virtue of their talent and 'too delicious' wit.

> Leading lights included Elisabeth Ponsonby, Brenda Dean Paul, the Jungman sisters, Bryan Guinness, Brian Howard, brothers Stephen and David Tennant, novelists Anthony Powell and Beverley Nichols, the Mitford sisters (including Nancy and Diana), and the actress Tallulah Bankhead.

Getting Together

The Bright Young People came together through a variety of exclusive social connections. Many, like Elizabeth Ponsonby and the Jungman sisters, met at public school. Eton in particular produced a huge proportion of the set, including Harold Acton, Brian Howard and Oliver Messel, while other public schools, such as Lancing, produced the likes of Evelyn Waugh and Tom Driberg.

Still more connections were made at Oxford University, where the vast majority of the male members of the 'Guinness set' studied.

Hearts and Hypocrites

At Oxford, Brian Howard's tight-knit group of friends were known as the Hearts, and included the sons of several noblemen as well as aspiring writers, among them Evelyn Waugh. The same group were also members of the renowned Hypocrites Club, an elite bunch of highly fashionable intellectuals who were only too aware of their social superiority.

The undergraduate magazine, *Isis*, described their flamboyant dress and 'entertaining' lifestyles but concluded: 'To talk to they are rather alarming. They have succeeded in picking up a whole series of intellectual catch-phrases with which they proceed to dazzle their friends and frighten their acquaintances: and they are the only people I have ever met who have reduced rudeness to a fine art.'

Who's That Boy? Brian Howard

Famous For: Socialite, fashionista and poet, Brian gained a reputation as one of the most outrageous and influential members of the Bright Young People.

Career Notes: At school he was a founding member of the Eton Society of the Arts, along with Anthony Powell, Harold Acton and novelist Henry Yorke, and a member of the famed Hypocrites Club at Oxford. A flamboyant homosexual, he was the life and soul of the party and behind many of the practical jokes and outrageous outings of the inner set.

Sound Bite: Daphne Weymouth, Marchioness of Bath, described him as 'a sinister impresario, with epigrams cracking from his lips and dark eyebrows raised, he looked mockingly down his nose at his protégés dancing like puppets as he pulled the strings'.

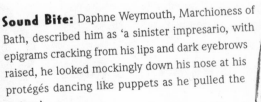

A Social Whirl

When education was done, the various emerging strands of the Bright Young People came together in London and – through mutual friends, family connections and prized invitations to 'frightfully' exclusive parties – joined together in one boisterous gaggle of youthful exuberance.

Introductions were made over lunches, teas and dinners as the fun-seeking crowd – most of whom had no need of regular paid employment – sought out ever more interesting people to add to their list of friends. In a single week in the 1927 diary of Eddie Gathorne-Hardy, quoted in D J Taylor's *Bright Young People*, he lists tea with 'Babe' Plunkett-Greene, lunch with Brian Howard, a party hosted by David Tennant and no less than five dinner engagements, including one at Tennant's Gargoyle Club and another at the exclusive French restaurant, Boulestin, which opened that year.

What's in a Name?

Barbara Cartland, who was eighteen in 1920, was the daughter of an army officer killed at Flanders; her mother owned a high-class dress store in London. As a socialite and society gossip columnist in the early twenties, she knew the set well and thought the moniker was an apt one. 'The Bright Young People was really an extremely good name for us,' she wrote in her autobiography. 'We were bright, we were gay, we were original and we did enjoy ourselves.'

But not all society figures embraced the nickname, and some deliberately distanced themselves from it. According to D J Taylor's book, *Bright Young People*, Bryan Guinness, the heir to the brewing fortune who would marry Diana Mitford in 1929, once complained that a society rag had 'implied that we belonged to a set called the Bright Young People ... I remember at the time suggesting that the set was entirely alien to us and our friends, and even suggesting that the appellation was libellous.'

The Paper Chase

CHASING CLUES – NEW SOCIETY GAME

MIDNIGHT CHASE IN LONDON

FIFTY MOTORCARS

THE BRIGHT YOUNG PEOPLE

A *Daily Mail* report in 1924 described a treasure hunt across London as a meet of 'the Society of Bright Young People'. The article described couples tearing across the capital in cars, hunting for clues and a final cash prize, calling it a craze that has 'captured all smart London'.

In fact, the fashion for treasure hunts had been growing in popularity for a year or two, ever since Zita Jungman and Lady Eleanor Smith raced across London on buses and tubes, leaving written clues behind them as to their next destination while their friends followed five minutes behind. The game proved such fun that others joined in and 'we used to amuse ourselves on blank afternoons by chasing each other around London'.

Hot Pursuit

At the start of the hunt, each player put a stake of around ten shillings into the pot and the winning pair received the lot, which was often as much as £100. The original creators found ingenious ways of hiding clues: the legendary Jungman sisters, Zita and Baby, once had a clue baked into a loaf of brown bread at the Hovis factory and even persuaded Lord Beaverbrook to print a fake edition of the *Evening Standard* with a clue hidden among made-up news stories.

Palace Pranks

Loelia Ponsonby remembered one occasion when the party descended on Buckingham Palace, much to the amusement of her father, Frederick, who worked for the Royal household:

> *We bore down on the sleeping Palace with screeching tyres, jumped out of our cars and rushed up and down the railings looking for the clue in the sentry boxes and shouting and screaming while all the time more cars were arriving. Next day my father came home with the story of extraordinary things that had happened at Buckingham Palace the night before; swarms of lunatics had tried to break in, the Captain of the Guard had turned out every available man, had telephoned for reinforcements and, suddenly, the whole crowd had disappeared as mysteriously as they arrived . . .*

Social Scavengers

The treasure hunts led to other amusements, in particular the 'scavenger' hunt. Each pair had to obtain certain items before reaching their designated finishing point and some of the objects required considerable bravado and some excellent connections. 'Scavenger parties became the vogue, which meant we made more of a nuisance of ourselves rather than just being noisy,' wrote Barbara Cartland in her memoir, and she described one particular occasion when she was taken on a hunt with a young suitor. 'The first object we collected was the cap of the commissionaire at the Ritz; the next a nameplate from one of the embassies; then we searched a mews for a horse's bridle. We searched and searched but we couldn't find one.'

One famous scavenger hunt included a red hair from an actress, a policeman's helmet and a pipe that had been smoked by Prime Minister Stanley Baldwin.

The Jungman Sisters

The beautiful Jungman sisters were at the heart of the Bright Young People and enjoyed a celebrated status among the smart set for their inventive escapades. Zita and Teresa, who was known as 'Baby', despite her own protests, were the daughters of Dutch artist Nico Jungman and the stepdaughters of Richard Guinness. Mum Beatrice was renowned for her parties, where the cream of society mixed with artists and actresses: Cecil Beaton remembered one particular event in 1926 where tables were laden with caviar, oysters, paté, turkeys, kidneys and bacon, hot lobsters and meringues, and the guests included Ivor Novello, actresses Gladys Cooper and Tallulah Bankhead, and artist Oliver Messel.

Photographing the two sisters lying head to head on a floor covered with cellophane, in the same year, Cecil included them in his *Book of Beauties*, in which he wrote:

> *The Jungman sisters are a pair of decadent eighteenth-century angels made of wax, exhibited at Madame Tussaud's before the fire. Baby is particularly waxy, and like a white gloxinia, with her Devonshire cream pallor and limpid mauve eyes. She has a waxen buttony nose and buttony lips, and her hair, spun of the flimsiest canary-bird silkiness, has a habit of falling lankly over her eyes, whence it is thrown back with a beguiling shrug of the head. Zita has the same smooth polished complexion and shoulders, and unearthly hollow voice, but she has a serpent-like little nose and there is great architectural strength and firmness about her jaw and mouth.*

With her smooth fringes and rather flat head, like a silky coconut, like a medieval page, and with her swinging gait, she looks very gallant, very princely. But she can, if she wishes, easily become a snake-like beauty, with a mysterious smile and a cold glint in her upward slanting eyes, though it is more than likely that she will impersonate to perfection a charming village maiden laughing deliciously up an apple tree.

Jolly Japes

Zita and Teresa, along with their old school friend Lady Eleanor Smith, were fond of charades and tricks ...

- On one occasion Teresa pretended to be a journalist and interviewed writer Beverley Nichols at Claridge's, while Zita and Lady Eleanor hid under a table.

- Teresa also dressed up as a Russian refugee she called 'Madame Anna Vorolsky', with a black wig and mink coat, and went around telling stories of the Red Terror while feigning hardship and pretending to sell her mother's jewels.

- While on holiday in Ascot in the early twenties, Eleanor and friends Brian Howard and Allanah Harper broke into the nearby country house of the Jungmans' mother and stepfather, where they threw a flannel nightdress belonging to the wife of the former Prime Minister, Mrs Asquith, on the fire before stealing Beatrice Guinness's pearls.

'The next day rumours were heard that Mrs Guinness' pearls were missing, the police had been called, and the search begun,' wrote Allanah in her memoirs. 'We confessed to Lura Howard (Brian's mother) who telephoned to the Guinness'. We returned the necklace and were severely reprimanded by Mrs Benjamin Guinness (Beatrice having retired to bed with a nervous collapse).'

At one garden party, which Teresa Jungman attended in the guise of her Russian royal, she met a respected general and his wife and announced to the general that she would never forget the night she had spent with him in Paris. When he replied, rather crossly, that he had only spent one night in Paris during the war, she quipped, 'Zat was zee night.'

From Scavenger to Scandal

The relative innocence of the Jungman japes were soon eclipsed in the gossip pages by the more scandalous antics of some of their more outrageous friends, led by the incorrigible Elizabeth Ponsonby and her openly camp cohorts, most notably Brian Howard. Their antics included illegal drinking at underground nightclubs, fake weddings and outrageous fancy dress parties, which sent shock waves through polite society.

Who Are Those Girls? Zita and Teresa 'Baby' Jungman

— ★ —

Famous For: Being at the heart of the Bright Young People and celebrated for their inventive escapades.

— ★ —

Career Notes: The well-connected Jungman sisters were the daughters of Nico Jungman and the stepdaughters of Richard Guinness. Their mother Beatrice was a famous socialite, and the girls inherited her love of fun. They enjoyed dressing up to play pranks and were behind the first London paper chase, starting a hugely popular trend. Evelyn Waugh was passionately in love with Teresa, and proposed on several occasions – to no avail.

— ★ —

Sound Bite: In later life, Zita commented to the *Independent* newspaper: 'We were all so over-excited. We were all talking about ourselves always.'

Who's That Girl? Elizabeth Ponsonby

— ★ —

Famous For: Daughter of politician Arthur Ponsonby, leading London socialite, and one of the founding members of the Bright Young People.

— ★ —

Career Notes: Along with her friends, Lady Eleanor Smith and Zita and Baby Jungman, she began the first paper chase across London. She also appeared as the bride in a mock wedding ceremony that became one of the most famous escapades of the Bright Young People and was behind the infamous 'bottle and bathing party' in 1928 (see page 42).

— ★ —

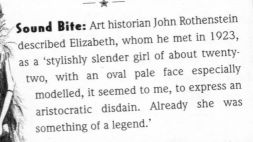

Sound Bite: Art historian John Rothenstein described Elizabeth, whom he met in 1923, as a 'stylishly slender girl of about twenty-two, with an oval pale face especially modelled, it seemed to me, to express an aristocratic disdain. Already she was something of a legend.'

Speak Easy

'If a few people got mobbed up and made fools of in the process [of our fun], well, it didn't really hurt them. We made a lot of other people laugh. Quite frankly, I think the Bright Young People brought a great deal of brightness to a world which was still sadly in need of it.'

From *We Danced All Night* by Barbara Cartland

Living Beyond Their Means

The pleasure-seeking life was expensive and not all the Bright Young People were as wealthy as they appeared. Elizabeth Ponsonby's mother Dorothea, for instance, was horrified by her daughter's extravagance. 'E's standard of riches angers me,' she wrote in her diary in 1923. 'Taxis always – everywhere. It doesn't amuse her to dine anywhere but at the Berkeley. She lives like a person with £3,000 a year who spends £800 on her dress.'

Family Ties

Loelia Ponsonby objected to being lumped in with her more outrageous cousin. In her autobiography, *Grace and Favour*, she wrote, 'The press made out that we were an organised gang who called ourselves the Bright Young People and that we found modern times so dull that we were deliberately trying to brighten them up ... They did not distinguish between us, the original Treasure Hunters, and the friends of my cousin Elizabeth. She organised parties which we thought exhibitionist – they always seemed to be held where there were photographers and where they would create the maximum disturbance.'

The Talk of the Town

The smart set in London developed their own language, affectations and baby talk to distinguish themselves from mainstream society. The faux-dramatic and over-exaggerated speech, caught beautifully for posterity by the novels of Evelyn Waugh and the plays and songs of Noël Coward, included such phrases as '*too* sick-making' and '*too* tired-making' with a liberal sprinkling of 'divine' and 'madly'.

A speech by a female character in Jocelyn Brooke's 1954 tale *Private View*, sums up the popular affectations and wild exaggerations of what he calls the 'pseudo-smart Bohemia' of the era:

> '*My Dear,*' *she exclaimed, in her fashionably husky voice,* '*it's utter heaven to see you. That monster Bertie Westmacott was meeting me, and I've been waiting here at least a thousand years, and I'm madly depressed. Do buy me a drink – here's some money, I know you're broke – and please introduce me to your boy-friend at once. I think he's a perfect lamb, and I'd like to eat him, do you think he'd mind?*'

Literary Inspiration

And it wasn't just the speech patterns of the Bright Young Things that Waugh was immortalising in his books. The characters in Waugh's novels are often thinly veiled portraits of his friends from the Roaring Twenties. The drama queen Agatha Runcible in *Vile Bodies* is thought to be inspired by Elizabeth Ponsonby, and gossip columnist Lord Simon Balcairn is based on Waugh's Oxford contemporary Patrick Balfour, later Lord Kinross, who wrote society gossip for the *Daily Sketch*. Teresa 'Baby' Jungman, with whom Waugh was fruitlessly in love, became Lady Julia Flyte in *Brideshead Revisited*, while Brian Howard was the inspiration for the camp and witty Anthony Blanche.

The sensitive Sebastian was a mixture of Waugh's two closest friends at Oxford, Alistair Graham and Hugh Patrick Lygon, the son of Earl Beaucham, and effeminate aesthete Stephen Tennant. Sebastian's relationship with his beloved teddy bear Aloysius, meanwhile, was prompted by John Betjeman's bear Archibold Ormsby-Gore.

Speak Easy

'You spend the first term at Oxford meeting interesting and exciting people and the rest of your time there avoiding them.'

Evelyn Waugh

Who's That Boy? Evelyn Waugh

— ★ —

Famous For: Novels such as *Brideshead Revisited*, *Vile Bodies* and *A Handful of Dust*, which drew heavily on the characters and experiences of the Bright Young People.

— ★ —

Career Notes: The son of a middle-class publisher, Evelyn was educated at Oxford, where he met many of the future Bright Young People and developed a taste for country house weekends and smart parties. He worked as a schoolmaster before publishing his first novel, *Decline and Fall*, in 1928. Although he was friends with many of the inner circle, Evelyn remained on the outskirts until the late 1920s, acting more as observer than participant.

— ★ —

Sound Bite: Loelia Ponsonby met the author at Great Cumberland Place, and recalled in *Grace and Favour*, 'Evelyn Waugh was a formidable young man who looked like a furious cherub. His glaring eye was watching us. His sharp ear missed nothing. What he said was pungent and he gave one the feeling that he was an unhappy man who found in the world "much to amuse but little to admire".'

Royal Seal of Approval

The Prince of Wales, who would later abdicate from the throne as King Edward VIII, was an unofficial patron of the Bright Young People. The dashing young Royal, who favoured Oxford bags, fast cars and polo, was a frequent guest at the cocktail parties in Mayfair and was often found in London's more exclusive nightclubs. His legendary drinking and womanising made him the ultimate star of the gossip columns but his hedonistic lifestyle also made him some enemies in court.

In his diaries Alan 'Tommy' Lascelles, who worked for the Prince's father George V, recorded how appalled he was by the heir to the throne's behaviour on a trip to Canada in 1927:

> *Before the end of our Canadian trip that year, I felt in such despair about him that I told Stanley Baldwin (then Prime Minister, and one of our party in Canada) that the Heir Apparent, in his unbridled pursuit of wine and women, and of whatever selfish whim occupied him at the moment, was going rapidly to the devil and would soon become no fit wearer of the British Crown.*

In fact, it was to be another affair, with the married American Wallis Simpson, which would see him abdicate from the throne nine years later. In the 1920s, however, he was at the height of his fun-loving, reckless youth, and became the perfect figurehead – and confederate – of the Bright Young Things.

'I WENT TO A MARVELLOUS PARTY'

> *It was the age of "parties". There were "white" parties in which we shot down to the country in fleets of cars, dressed in white from head to foot ... There were Mozart parties in which, powdered and peruked, we danced by candlelight and then – suddenly bored – rushed out into the street to join a gang excavating the gas main at Hyde Park Corner.*
>
> Beverley Nichols, *All I Could Never Be*

The 1920s were a time to throw caution and consideration to the wind and P-A-R-T-Y. As long as it was wild, decadent, completely over the top and exuberant, it was in. Themed celebrations became the order of the day, as the Bright Young Things discovered the age of revelry.

Evelyn Waugh's second novel, *Vile Bodies*, is a satire on the lifestyle of the Bright Young People. In the book, Waugh's hero,

Adam Fenwick-Symes, lists an array of lavish themed celebrations, many of which were actual events attended by the Mayfair set. Collectively known as 'freak parties', the gatherings became increasingly scandalous as each host vied to outdo the last.

> Evelyn Waugh dedicated *Vile Bodies* to Bryan Guinness and his wife, Diana Mitford. The couple were legendary hosts and, on being invited to one of their many events during the writing of the novel, Waugh wrote to his friend Henry Yorke: 'I might go up for it if I thought there wouldn't be anyone who wouldn't be too much like the characters in my new book.'

Dressing-up Box

After the thrill of the treasure hunt lost its novelty factor, the fancy dress party became the next big wheeze. David Tennant and his actress wife Hermione held a 'Mozart' party where the guests wore eighteenth-century dress and later presided over an Edwardian party, with invitees urged to 'come as you were twenty years ago'. Lady Dean Paul arrived in a 1906 dress pushing a pram which contained her adult daughter, Brenda, in baby clothes and the band was dressed in Eton suits and school caps.

39

In 1929, when the themed party was reaching fever pitch, the *Evening Standard* reported that 'some of the smartest and prettiest women in London have been searching for a dress appropriate for a Wild West party and cowboy costumes are at a premium'. This wild do at Harold Acton's Lancaster Gate home was followed by Brian Howard's twenty-fourth birthday, which he named The Great Urban Dionysia, urging his guests to visit the British Museum for inspiration for Greek costumes.

The Big Top

Up and coming designer Norman Hartnell – who went on to design the wedding dress of the future Queen Elizabeth – made his mark on the party circuit with a hugely extravagant 'Circus Party' in the summer of 1929. He rented a grand house in London's Bruton Street and invited 250 guests to come as circus characters. The house had been decorated as a fairground, with live circus animals, including a dancing bear, a seal and a wolf. The host was dressed as the ringmaster, while Brenda Dean Paul came as a female wrestler, Ivor Novello was dressed in a blue velvet sailor suit and Olivia Wyndham arrived with two live snakes coiled around her neck.

In *We Danced All Night,* Barbara Cartland recalled, 'There were performing wolves which skipped merrily round an arena, acrobats, a somewhat lethargic bear and other stunts.

'Eleanor (Smith) led her white pony, with a scarlet saddle and jingling with golden bells, up the stairs. But the Marchioness of Carisbrooke, wearing a riding habit of violet cloth and a top hat, left her horse outside.'

> The Prince of Wales was a devotee of the fancy dress party and introduced the idea that guests should be completely unrecognisable. He arrived at one shindig as Bonnie Prince Charlie and then changed to become a Chinese peasant. At another, thrown by the Duke and Duchess of Sutherland, at Mayfair's Hampden House, he and his brother Bertie, later King George VI, dressed up as baby boys.

The Impersonation Party

In the summer of 1927, one event was to shine a spotlight on the self-absorption and celebrity status of the Bright Young People. Captain Neil McLachlan held an Impersonation Party at his Brooke Street home and guests were asked to come dressed as a well-known personality. Quite a few of the trendier guests chose to come as each other. Elizabeth Ponsonby arrived in a red wig as actress and model Iris Tree, gossip columnist Tom Driberg slapped on make-up and drew on an arched eyebrow to become Brian Howard and Olivia Plunkett-Greene bleached her hair to resemble her fellow socialite Brenda Dean Paul.

The Party Went Swimmingly

The four brightest lights of the Bright Young People were joint hosts of arguably the most outrageous evening of them all – the Bath and Bottle Party. Babe Plunkett-Greene, Elizabeth Ponsonby, Eddie Gathorne-Hardy and Brian Howard hired St George's swimming baths in Buckingham Palace Road, asking guests to 'please wear a Bathing Suit and bring a bath towel and a Bottle'.

The party, which took place in the sweltering summer of 1928, caused uproar among the chattering classes – not least because of the hiring of a 'negro band'.

Speak Easy

'There were swimming parties where at midnight, we descended on some municipal baths hired for the occasion, and disported ourselves with an abandon that was all the fiercer because we knew that the press was watching – and watching with a very disapproving eye.'

From *All I Could Never Be* by Beverley Nichols

Read All About It

The *Sunday Chronicle* reported of the infamous event: 'Great astonishment and not a little indignation is being expressed in London over the revelation that in the early hours of yesterday morning a large number of society women were dancing in bathing dresses to the music of a negro band at a "swim and dance" gathering organised by some of Mayfair's Bright Young People.'

Tom Driberg, in the *Daily Express*'s 'Talk of London' column, gave an eyewitness account of the event, revealing that some revellers had two or three costumes that they changed into over the course of the evening, which began at 11 p.m. and went on until the early hours. 'Cocktails were served in the gallery,' he wrote, 'where the cocktail-mixers evidently found the heat intolerable, for they also donned bathing costumes at the earliest opportunity.'

When the police came to break things up the following morning, where the scantily clad guests were astonishing ordinary people on their way to work, some of the more spirited revellers attempted to drag the unfortunate officers into the changing room in the hope of disrobing them.

A special cocktail, christened the Bathwater Cocktail, was invented for the occasion.

It was one part Amaretto, one part blue curaçao, two parts cranberry juice, two parts pineapple juice, one part Southern Comfort.

Party-Poopers

Even those close to the Tennant brothers, Brian Howard and Elizabeth Ponsonby often found the parties a little too hot to handle. In *Brian Howard: Portrait of a Failure*, by Marie-Jaqueline Lancaster, Allanah Harper recalled:

> *The last party I went to with Brian at that period was one given by David Tennant. It ended in a free fight, I found myself in the middle of a jealous fracas, scuffle and scrimmage, which although it had nothing to do with me, resulted in my dress being practically torn off and tufts of my hair being held up as trophies. After that experience I never went to parties of this kind again.*

The Great Mayfair War

The rebellious shenanigans of the young set, designed as they were to upset social convention, had the desired effect among the more traditional hosts and hostesses. After the scramble and screeching tyres of the scavenger hunts and the hilarity of the costume parties came a trend for gatecrashing society balls, tagging along with a friend who had been officially invited.

This led to a stand-off dubbed 'The Great Mayfair War', after Lady Ellesmere, mistress of Bridgewater House, asked four guests she did not recognise – Stephen Tennant, David Plunkett-Greene, Elizabeth Lowndes and Cecil Beaton's sister Nancy – to leave.

The newspapers went to town, as Lady Ellesmere claimed that she was merely defending the right to open a home only to those you want to enter it. Stephen Tennant admitted to the *Evening Standard* that, although he and David had been invited, they brought some female friends along, a practice he saw as the norm. All would have been well, he believed, had his hostess not overheard Elizabeth telling another guest, 'Isn't this a joke, I have not been invited.'

The final fling

The Red and White Party, thrown in the house of dancer Maud Allan by the art dealer Arthur Jeffress, began at 11 p.m. on 21 November 1929 and was, according to John Montgomery's 1957 book, *The Twenties*, 'the last hectic party of the twenties, the party to end all parties, surpassing even the Wild West party and the Court party'.

The invitations, white on a bright scarlet background, were so sought after that many were stolen from mantelpieces and used by gatecrashers on the night. Guests at the 'monster ball' were instructed to wear only red and white and the host greeted them in a white sailor suit with red trimmings, white

> The red and white theme stretched to the lavish array of food available at the party. The spread included red caviar, lobsters, salmon, ham, apples, tomato salad, pink and red blancmanges, trifles and jellies. It also extended to drinks, with only champagne, white or red wine, or gin offered to guests, with no whisky available. Cigarettes, traditionally provided by hosts at the time, were displayed in red and white boxes.

gloves loaded with diamonds and a muff made of white narcissi. Three large rooms in the spacious house had been decorated, with the central space draped in swathes of scarlet and white cloth, a white room for a bar and a red room, complete with mattresses, for 'sitting out'.

The riotous party, which went on until dawn, ended with a few people stripping off and one girl – apparently Brenda Dean Paul – being prevented from pulling the hair of another young beauty as they clashed at the drinks table. Montgomery observed: 'The girl was wearing only a choker of pearls and a large red and white spotted handkerchief fixed around her middle by a thin white belt. People wearing more clothes found it almost unbearably hot.'

Montgomery's report suggests that the cost of the party was £500 – around £25,000 today.

Speak Easy

'Some guests mixed the drinks and gulped them down; then mixed their dancing partners. The huge room became a medley of red and white sailor suits, white dresses and sashes, red wigs, long white kid gloves, pink hats, and even false red noses. Red and white "nuns" danced with men dressed as exotic birds with elaborate feather headdresses, men danced stripped to the waist, wearing red sailors' bell-bottom trousers; a man dressed as Queen Elizabeth, wearing a red wig, sat in the hall solemnly playing "Abide With Me" on the organ.'

From *The Twenties* by John Montgomery

Porter Parties

The red and white theme may have been influenced by an earlier ball thrown by the popular composer Cole Porter and his wife Linda in Venice. The couple spent much of the twenties in the Italian city and also in Paris, where their lavish parties were legendary.

In the summer of 1926, they rented the Palazzo Rezzonico, where they threw their most spectacular ball. Hundreds of

guests were ferried to the historic palace by gondolieri in red and white costumes. At midnight, the music stopped and they were directed into a grand salon, where red and white costumes of papier-mâché had been provided. After dressing in the costumes, the guests returned to the ballroom to dance, creating a dramatic spectacle.

One guest, Prince Faucigny-Lucinge, was quoted in William McBrien's biography of Cole Porter as saying, 'I recall a tight-rope dancer, such as there were then still on the piazza, keeping all eyes riveted on him crossing over from the top of the illuminated courtyard, dressed in white and red, and with table and chair, affecting to have a meal over the anguished guests.'

The same year the Porters also took over an ornate domed barge owned by the Excelsior Hotel – and converted it into a jazz club with capacity for 150 people. They brought a jazz orchestra out from Paris to play on the *Arca di Noe*, led by Leslie 'Hutch' Hutchinson (see page 186). While Hutch was kept on to play at parties throughout the summer, the converted vessel made only one journey.

The End of the Party

By the end of the decade the 'freak parties' had become a source of ridicule in the satirical press, with *Punch* columns making fun of the 'Dull Young People', and had caused some concern among the more polite ladies' journals. In the summer of 1929, *The Lady*'s columnist 'Johanna' asked, 'Has the freak party reached the point at which it becomes both an absurdity and a nuisance?' The blatantly public 'high spirits' of the events, she argued, had even become 'a source of annoyance to the young'.

FASHION IN A FLAP

Fashion is not something that exists in dresses only. Fashion is in the sky, in the street, fashion has to do with ideas, the way we live, what is happening.

Coco Chanel

The fashion of the Roaring Twenties is, quite simply, iconic. Summoning up an entire decade of flirty fun and freedom with a flick of a tasselled skirt and a coy look on a bob-framed face, the dropped waistlines, boyish figures and – imagine! – trouser-suited strumpets of the 1920s changed the face of fashion forever.

The Roaring Twenties brought about revolution for women in the Western world – and not least in the style stakes. After the austere and hard-working years of the First World War, young women found a new independence, and decided it was time to let their hair down.

Bob's Your Uncle

For the fashion-forward, this now meant cutting their hair short – very short. The liberated woman of the jazz age wore her hair in a fashionable bob: either straight and glossy, or 'shingled', meaning cut shorter at the nape of the neck in a V-shape. This shorter style caused outrage in the newspapers, spawning headlines such as 'Shingle Blow to Marriage' and 'Shingles Leave Girls Single'.

In her autobiography, Barbara Cartland recalled one of the Bright Young People sending shock waves through Oxford with the latest fashion: 'When Patrick Balfour was at Oxford in 1923, Elizabeth Ponsonby (daughter of the Under Secretary of State for Foreign Affairs in the Socialist Government) came down to display her shingled head. "It was the first shingle I had seen," he said, "and it induced in me a feeling of astonishment coupled with faint horror. I was, in fact, shocked!"'

Shock Waves

It's difficult to overestimate how alarming society found the new hairstyle, which was as much a statement of feminism as a new look. Engagements foundered on the very snip of the hairdressers' scissors and a huge debate raged over the cut. Irene Castle, a popular ballroom dancer credited with introducing the bob to American women, defended her style – and its results – in an article published in the *Ladies' Home Journal* in 1921:

There has been so much controversy over the bobbed-hair craze that I feel I ought to put some of the world right, as to my side of it at least. I do not claim to be the first person to wear bobbed hair; in fact, I believe there are a number of people who, like myself, picture Joan of Arc with shorn locks! There have been several periods in history when women wore short hair. It is easier to be the first person to do a thing than the first to introduce it, and I believe I am largely blamed for the homes wrecked and engagements broken because of clipped tresses. I do not wish to take the blame, because in a great number of cases I find the responsibility a serious one and the results a 'chamber of horrors'.

To Bob or Not to Bob?

Actress Mary Pickford gave the opposite view in the 1927 issue of *Pictorial Review*, entitled 'Why I Have Not Bobbed Mine': 'In the epidemic of hair-cutting which has swept the country I am one of the few who have escaped. That does not mean that I have been inoculated by the germ, but that I have resisted valiantly. It has been a hard-fought battle, and the problem has occupied many of my waking and sleeping hours. I say "sleeping" because it often intrudes itself into my dreams.'

After arguing that cutting her hair might have an impact on her career, she continues, 'Then there is my family to consider. I think I should never be forgiven by my mother, my husband, or my maid if I should commit the indiscretion of cutting my hair. The last in particular seems to take a great personal pride in its length and texture, and her horror-stricken face whenever I mention the possibility of cutting it makes me pause and consider.' Two years later, though, she was to succumb to the scissors (see page 150).

Simple But Effective

There was a revolution under way in women's wardrobes, too. Out went the long feminine dresses, fussily trimmed with bows and lace, and in came the simpler style of the flapper dress. Women's formerly prized 'hourglass' figures disappeared underneath tubular dresses with dropped waistbands, while the slightly shorter hemline, which reached the mid-calf, allowed for much more freedom of movement.

Fabulous Fashion Design

The emphasis in fashion design moved from the bolstered bust of the Edwardian era to the hips, with sashes or blocks of colour highlighting the dropped waistline, and decorative detail, such as fabric flowers, placed to one side.

The skirts of the dress were pleated or tiered for daywear and often fringed for the evening, causing a fabulous effect during the all-night dance marathons that were all the rage. The simple sheath dresses were jazzed up with elaborate beading, sequins and tiny mirrors sewn onto the fabric, creating shimmering visions as the Bright Young Things went about their business.

What a Boob!

The smart young women-about-town – described by Barbara Cartland as 'enchanting, sexless, bosomless, hipless, thighless creatures' – favoured a curve-free, youthful figure. To achieve the desired effect the corset, which had long strained to create the womanly curves of the Victorian and Edwardian era, was ditched in favour of the looser camisole and brassiere (which, in the twenties, offered no support).

As a result, ladies with larger busts took to bandaging their breasts to flatten and contain them, using tubular, elasticated roll-on underwear to keep everything in place. The Symington Side Lacer, which could be laced up under both arms and tightened to compress the bust, was a popular innovation. Those born with slighter figures could, of course, get away with a simple lace bandeau or camisole.

Speak Easy

'The dresses of the twenties involved the designers in an arduous and exhausting struggle against nature. It was the battle of the brassiere in reverse and half the dressmaker's time was spent in making intricate contraptions of canvas and elastic to be fitted tightly over any bust that showed signs of intransigence. To own a bust in the twenties was extremely déclassé.'

Norman Hartnell discusses a designer's trials with Beverley Nichols in *The Sweet and Twenties*

A Stockinged Leg

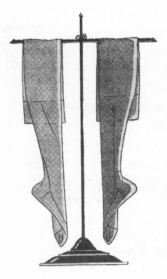

At the start of the decade stockings were dark wool or cotton, and rolled down to just above the knee or slightly below. But the introduction of artificial silk, named rayon, in 1924 brought about a new nude style, with beige, cream and light brown tones giving a more natural look and showing legs to their best advantage.

To reduce the shine of the synthetic stockings, the girls would powder their legs before leaving for a night out.

Speak Easy

'When I first came out we wore beige, grey, black or white stockings. I remember the first time I saw a woman walking down the street in flesh-coloured ones. She was wearing a black dress that drooped at the back and was short in front, and I thought she looked quite extraordinary and just like an ostrich.'

Loelia Ponsonby in her autobiography,
Grace and Favour

Daring to Bare

The frivolous new style meant that more flesh was on show than ever before. Many of the evening dresses were sleeveless and the more daring socialites risked plunging necklines or backs. The nude effect could also be achieved by the use of sheer materials, such as silk, organza and chiffon, creating a softer look around the shoulders and arms. Hemlines, however, stayed relatively modest, covering as far as the calf — until 1926, when they crept daringly above the knee.

Jazzing It Up

The simple, drop-waisted dresses could be glammed up for outings with a number of must-have accessories. Art Nouveau designs were de rigueur and the emphasis shifted to design rather than the value of decorative items.

Fancy Footwork

As dancing was the key to a flapper's lifestyle, high heels were out of the question. Shoes were fairly low, with practical yet modish Cuban or Louis-style (hourglass shape) heels, and

straps or T-bars across the arch of the foot, similar to those worn by professional Latin and ballroom dancers today.

Head Case

The wide-brimmed hats of the previous generation were replaced with close-fitting cloche hats that were pulled low over one's ears.

For the evening, a simple band was often worn as a stylish accessory, perhaps with a feather or flower for decoration, or sprinkled with sparkling beads.

Divine Finery

A long string of pearls was an essential item in the society flapper's arsenal and looked perfect with the flat-fronted dresses. Fashion-conscious girls on a budget, however, could make do with beads, always worn in long strands. Earrings were also worn long and dangly and brooches, sporting feathers and colourful stones, were a popular addition to coats and jackets. At the high end of the market, coral, jade, aquamarine, onyx and opal replaced the more classic diamonds, and platinum was the latest luxury metal.

Long gloves often accompanied the sleeveless dresses, while long cigarette holders provided an elegant accessory for the girl about town. Feathers were all the rage; the smarter set carrying a fan of ostrich feathers to cool down in the evening.

In Paris, outrageous flapper Josephine Baker caused a stir when she appeared in the 1927 French film, *La Revue des Revues*, wearing a feather plume, beaded panties ... and very little else.

Lipstick and Powder

Before the twenties, the use of heavy make-up was considered vulgar outside the theatre, but the rebellious youngsters embraced the outlandish look. Thick dark kohl was used around the eyes, with copious mascara employed for the long-lashed look. Powdered faces were finished off with vampish red lipstick and eyelids were made to shine with Vaseline.

Metal lipstick-holders had come onto the market in 1915, meaning they could be easily carried in a handbag. For the first time ever, it became fashionable to touch up make-up in public, with girls fishing out compacts and lip colour wherever they sat in the dance halls and tearooms.

Twenties film star Clara Bow inspired a craze for the cupid bow lips in the mid-twenties, with her deep red, perfectly sculpted mouth. The look, created by Max Factor from his newly developed Color Harmony range, led to the brand becoming a popular choice with young women, along with Elizabeth Arden.

Who's That Girl? Clara Bow

Famous For: The American actress was dubbed 'The It Girl' after starring in a movie called *It* (1927) and she epitomised the wild and seductive flapper.

Career Notes: She played her first flapper in the 1923 movie *Painted People* and went on to play more in such movies as *The Perfect Flapper* and *Black Oxen*.

Sound Bite: Director Frank Lloyd, who cast Bow as high-society flapper Janet Oglethorpe in *Black Oxen*, commented: 'Bow is the personification of the ideal aristocratic flapper: mischievous, pretty, aggressive, quick-tempered and deeply sentimental.'

In 1920, Max Factor's son Frank persuaded his father to call his products 'make-up' rather than cosmetics. Until then, the term, derived from the verb 'to make up one's face', had been rejected as belonging to the theatre and people of 'dubious reputation'.

Coco Chanel

The French designer Coco Chanel was the most influential style icon of the decade. As Joshua Zietz put it in his book *Flapper*, Chanel was 'the right woman, at the right time, in the right place'. Her 'garçonne' look, created in Paris, soon caught on around the world and inspired the boyish style of the flapper age.

Irritated by the frills and frou-frou of the upper-class female wardrobe, and conscious of the need for practical clothing for women who had worked through the war years and beyond, Chanel set about simplifying haute couture. Using soft jersey, the traditional material for men's underwear, she produced elegant suits, cardigans and trousers, as well as beaded evening dresses with simple shapes and dropped waistbands. Coco said she came up with the look because she felt it was time to 'let go of the waistline'.

The Chanel suit was heralded as 'the new uniform for afternoon and evening'.

Who's That Girl? Coco Chanel

Famous For: Revolutionising the fashion world.

Career Notes: In 1921, Coco launched her first perfume, which she named after her lucky number. Chanel No. 5 has been a bestseller ever since. Five years later, she caused a new revolution when she introduced her 'Little Black Dress'. For the first time, the hemline rose daringly above the knee.

Sound Bite: In 1923 she told *Harper's Bazaar*: 'Simplicity is the keynote of all true elegance.'

In 1926, American *Vogue* referred to the Little Black Dress as 'Chanel's Ford', meaning it was as popular and as universally available as Henry Ford's mass-produced motorcar.

Bright Young Men

Before the First World War, young men had adopted similar cuts of suit to their older counterparts – but the jazz age was all about the celebration of youth, and the Bright Young Things had no intention of dressing like their dads. The formal frock coats and morning suits of a bygone age were replaced with more relaxed lounge suits, worn with or without a tie, and often featuring zips rather than buttons, as this marvellously practical new technology made itself indispensable to designers.

A well-tailored tuxedo fitted the bill for eveningwear, often worn with a modish two-tone lace-up brogue, which became highly fashionable with those chaps who liked to flash their feet while dancing the Charleston.

Towards the end of the decade, attached collars began to be worn in place of the starched detachable ones of the past, and this relic of the Edwardian era slowly had its day.

Knickerbocker Glory

Men's casual wear in the twenties was influenced by the popularity of hearty outdoor sports, such as golf, tennis and shooting. As a result, knickerbockers, soon shortened to 'knickers', became popular casual wear for the well-dressed gentleman.

Worn with a Norfolk coat – traditionally used for shooting, due to its pleated back for ease of movement – the knickers came in four styles: plus-fours, plus-sixes, plus-eights and plus-tens. The number denoted how many inches below the knee the trouser leg stopped.

In Zelda Fitzgerald's account of the couple's travels, *Show Mr and Mrs F to Number*—, she wrote: 'At the O. Henry in Greensville they thought a man and his wife ought not to be dressed alike in white knickerbockers in 1920, and we thought the water in the tubs ought not to run red mud.'

In 1925, as a way around the banning of knickers in the university, a group of Oxford undergraduates came up with a new loose style of flannel trouser. Considered outrageous by the establishment, the Oxford bags — so named for their baggy legs — could measure between 22 and 40 inches at the bottom of the leg and, as a result, could be slipped over the offending knickerbockers with ease.

Suits You, Sir!

While the trendsetters at university were cutting new cloth with their Oxford bags, the boys of Eton still dressed as if they were on their way to a wedding, in top hat and tails and starched white shirts. The Eton suit became a fashionable look for boys throughout Britain.

The name of the school also lent itself to a style of short bob, adopted by daring flappers and called the Eton Crop.

Gone for a Burton

The 1920s saw the launch of ready-made suits (as opposed to the costly bespoke variety), which became available in Burton Menswear, a chain of shops originally founded by Montague Burton in 1903.

The concept was a hit. By the end of the 1920s, there were 400 'Burtons' in Britain, offering a cheap and accessible alternative to the expensive tailored suits favoured by the wealthy.

Speak Easy

'Though we were not particularly rich, we were dressed in some style. Every young man with some pretensions to gentility possessed not only a dinner jacket but a tailcoat ... However hard up we were, we all seemed to have gold cigarette cases, even if they were quite small, and nine carat, and purchased in Regent Street.'

From *The Sweet and Twenties* by Beverley Nichols

Fashion for All

And this accessibility wasn't just limited to the chaps – as with so many other aspects of life in the twenties, the girls were getting in on the act too. High fashion had long been the preserve of the rich, with the cost of fine fabrics and dressmakers putting haute couture out of reach of the masses. Only the wealthy could invest in the expensive, glamorous dresses seen at debutante balls and dinner parties, and however much the servant girls and middle classes might sigh with envy at the glorious style of society women, their lofty sartorial ambitions were doomed to remain daydreams.

But that was until the 1920s. This decade saw the rise of cheaper off-the-peg womenswear, in stores such as the Co-op and in smaller independent shops in the high street. Affordable women's magazines and easy-to-make dress patterns also led to a boom in home-dressmaking and knitting. At long last, the ordinary girl could realistically aspire to style *and* make it happen — and she did so with gusto and with practical application.

Off-the-Peg

In a series of interviews compiled by the Ambleside Oral History Group, an unnamed lady recalled her twice-yearly trip to buy clothes in the 1920s, and the must-have items of the day:

> *By this time, the dressmaker had stopped coming, and we wore clothes which we bought off-the-peg, as it were, from shops. My father discovered a little shop down in London and we went there and bought a lot of clothes once or twice a year ...*
>
> *The fashion was still for shapeless dresses, but summer dresses had rather more shape: they were sleeveless and made of prettier colours. Chiffon dresses were very pretty in pale greens and yellows, and we wore satin dance dresses as well.*
>
> *For important balls, we had white elbow-length gloves, and we bought white satin shoes, which we dyed to match the exact shade of the dress.*

Bronzed Beauties

In 1923, Coco Chanel caused a sensation by acquiring – and flaunting – a deep suntan. For the first time ever, tans – once shunned as the sign of manual labour – became fashionable, first in Paris and then worldwide, and the new look changed the face of summer forever.

As befits the age of the flapper, swimming costumes got skimpier and shrank from a cover-all bloomer design to a more daring one-piece.

Speak Easy

'The Flapper ... wore a one-piece bathing suit because she had a good figure, she covered her face with powder and paint because she didn't need it and she refused to be bored chiefly because she wasn't boring. She was conscious that the things she did were the things she had always wanted to do.'

From 'Eulogy on the Flapper' by Zelda Fitzgerald, published in *Metropolitan* magazine, 1922

Oh, I Do Like to Be Beside the Seaside

For the chic and wealthy, the French Riviera and the Italian resorts now became the holiday destinations of choice, while for the majority beaches closer to home provided a break from it all. With suntans now a popular trend, those who could afford it would happily traipse off to the coast for a week or two of sun and sand, and the seaside became the place to be during the hot summer months.

Speak Easy

'Mother, father and we four youngest girls, plus Edith, one of the maids, travelled there by train ... There were two beaches to play on. We wore cotton gingham dresses which we tucked into matching knickers when we went paddling. We never went swimming in the sea.'

Nancy Emery recalls regular fortnights at the coast in Scarborough in *The Early Twentieth Century (When I Was Young)*

Fashion Forward

Perhaps the most striking thing about twenties fashion is that it wasn't just about clothes. It was the statement that set the young apart from the old, the rich from the poor and the 'respectable' aristocracy from the Bright Young People. It was a sartorial rebellion and a visible proof that the wearer was a fully signed-up member of what F Scott Fitzgerald called the 'jazz age'.

COCKTAIL HOUR

‘The only things that the United States has given to the world are skyscrapers, jazz, and cocktails. That is all. And in Cuba, in our America, they make much better cocktails.’

Federico García Lorca

Having got closer to their American cousins during the First World War, the younger generation now thrilled to the delights of the jazz age – the bobbed hair, the flapper dresses, lipstick, cinema and, of course, cocktails.

The exotic mixtures soared in popularity in the twenties, when alcohol was banned in the States and illegally distilled spirits had to be drowned in fruit juices, cream and soda to make them vaguely palatable. While the Prohibition law, passed in 1919, succeeded in reducing the overall consumption of liquor, it also gave booze a new glamour. The brightly coloured cocktails, with their olive garnish and fancy straws, became the illicit pleasure of those 'in the know' and underground clubs, or speakeasies, sprung up all over the States, allowing organised crime to flourish on the vast profits.

An Englishman Abroad

Author and journalist Beverley Nichols sampled the delights of the speakeasy on a trip to the US in 1928. According to Lucy Moore's *Anything Goes,* he wrote:

Prohibition has set many dull feet dancing ... The disappearance of the 'speakeasy' would be an infinite loss to all romanticists. Who, having slunk down the little flight of stairs into the area, glancing to right and left, in order to make sure no police are watching, having blinked at the sudden lighted grille and assured the proprietor, whose face peers through the bars, of his bona fides – who would willingly forfeit these delicious preliminaries? And who, having taken his seat in the shuttered restaurant, having felt all the thrill of the conspirator, having jumped at each fresh ring of the bell, having, perhaps, enjoyed the supreme satisfaction of taking part in a real raid – who would prefer, to these excitements, a sedate and legal dinner, even if the wines of the world were at his disposal?

Bathtubs . . .

Whisky and gin brewed in outhouses and back rooms kept the bars of the speakeasies flowing. The clear spirits distilled from cheap grain alcohol, with added water and juniper berries, or glycerine, became known as 'bathtub gin'.

Despite popular belief, the alcohol wasn't fermented in a bathtub at all. It actually referred to the fact that the bottle used was too tall to be filled from a tap in the sink, so it had to be topped up with water from the tap in the bath.

. . . and Bootlegs

At the same time a lucrative trade in 'rum-running' sprang up, with smugglers bringing in cheap rum from the Caribbean. Many soon realised higher profits could be made by smuggling Canadian whisky, British gin and French champagne, keeping the likes of the fizz-loving Fitzgeralds expensively sozzled.

Pirate Captain Bill McCoy made a fortune from smuggling Caribbean rum into the States, via the Atlantic ocean. The bottles he delivered, being of the highest quality brands, became known as 'the real McCoy'.

What's Your Poison?

Underground drinking brought many risks, and not just of being busted. Some of the concoctions were more likely to put you in a hospital bed than a police cell. Here are a few of the most toxic tipples of the era:

Yack Yack bourbon – burnt sugar and iodine made in Chicago, where Al Capone ruled the roost. Burned the throat rather than quenching a thirst.

Panther whisky – with a high concentration of fuel oil this could put a tiger in your tank. In fact, it was thought to trigger hallucination, sexual depravity, paranoia and murderous impulses.

Applejack – an apple brandy distilled from cider by leaving to freeze and removing ice chunks. This method resulted in dangerously high levels of methanol and ethanol.

Soda Pop Moon – a strong Moonshine created in Philadelphia from rubbing alcohol, commonly used as a disinfectant.

Jackass whisky – distilled from fruit, sugar and wheat, it was known to cause internal bleeding.

Jake – a fluid extract of Jamaican ginger, at over 70 per cent proof, the liquor caused paralysis and often death. The dragging gait of a partially paralysed user became known as 'The Jake Walk' or 'Jake Leg'.

Borderline Humour

On a trip to the Commonwealth country of Canada, the Prince of Wales heard a humorous ditty about the Prohibition which he delighted in relaying to his father, King George V:

> *Four and twenty Yankees, feeling very dry,*
> *Went across the border to get a drink of rye.*
> *When the rye was opened, the Yanks began to sing,*
> *'God bless America, but God save the King!'*

Cocktails for Two

Renowned author Fitzgerald was roaring drunk for most of the Roaring Twenties. Cocktail parties feature heavily in his books, in particular *The Great Gatsby*, which centres on the high living of the wealthy Long Island set, and he and wife Zelda were never far from a gin fizz or a bottle of bubbly.

In *Show Mr and Mrs F to Number——*, a joint account of their travels in Europe, the couple recorded a 1924 trip to France: 'The Hotel du Cap at Antibes was almost deserted. The heat of day lingered in the blue and white blocks of the balcony and from the great canvas mats our friends had spread along the terrace we warmed our sunburned backs and invented new cocktails.'

Speak Easy

'The bar is in full swing, and floating rounds of cocktails permeate the garden outside, until the air is alive with chatter and laughter, and casual innuendo and introductions forgotten on the spot, and enthusiastic meetings between women who never knew each other's names.'

From *The Great Gatsby* by F Scott Fitzgerald

Gin Rickey

Fitzgerald's preferred tipple was gin and his favourite cocktail was a 'Gin Rickey', made with lime juice:

> 2 fl. oz gin
> ¾ fl. oz lime juice
> Soda
> Slice of lime

Pour the gin and lime juice into a chilled highball glass filled with ice cubes. Top with club soda, and stir gently. Garnish with the slice of lime.

In Paris, the Fitzgeralds' love of cocktails led to a mishap with their daughter Scottie, then three.

'We bathed the daughter in the bidet by mistake and she drank the gin fizz thinking it was lemonade and ruined the luncheon table next day.'

Who's That Boy? F Scott Fitzgerald

— ★ —

Famous For: Bestselling novels including *The Great Gatsby, Tender is the Night* and *The Beautiful and the Damned*.

— ★ —

Career Notes: A penniless author when he fell for eighteen-year-old Zelda at a country club in Montgomery, Fitzgerald married her after his first novel, *This Side of Paradise*, was published in 1920. The couple became the most dazzling celebrities of the decade and their exploits at parties — jumping into fountains, getting spectacularly drunk and starting fights in Harlem dance halls — afforded them legendary status. They were considered by many as the most beautiful couple of the era, and Dorothy Parker, who first encountered them hitching a lift on a taxi — Zelda on the bonnet and her husband on the roof — said they looked 'as if they had both stepped out of the sun'.

— ★ —

Sound Bite: Close friend Lillian Gish remarked, 'They didn't make the twenties, they *were* the twenties.'

The Orange Blossom

A favourite of Zelda Fitzgerald, the sugar in this cocktail masked the bitter taste of the bathtub gin:

> 2 fl. oz gin
> 1 fl. oz orange juice
> 1 tsp sugar
> 1 slice orange

Mix the gin, orange juice and sugar in a shaker half-filled with ice cubes. Shake well, and strain into a cocktail glass. Garnish with the slice of orange.

Pink Lady

A potentially lethal mixture of bathtub gin, applejack and egg white, this was another Fitzgerald favourite:

> ½ fl. oz gin
> 1 ½ fl. oz applejack
> Juice of half a lemon
> 1 fresh egg white
> 2 dashes grenadine

Shake all ingredients vigorously together with ice, strain into a chilled glass and garnish.

Shaken and Stirred

As the sweet whiff of cocktails wafted over the Atlantic, the Mayfair set adopted the new tipples with their usual gay abandon. Cocktail parties became the norm in the early twenties, to the arch disapproval of many of the more conservative middle

classes, who felt the influence of the Americans was going too far. The cocktail, like the short skirt and bobbed hair, was seen as a deliberate disregard for the old ways, and the start of a very slippery slope.

At a 'second childhood party', thrown by Rosemary Sanders at Rutland Gate in 1929, the guests arrived in prams, played on rocking horses in the garden and, according to the *Daily Express*, 'Cocktails were served in nursery mugs and the "bar" was a babies' pen.' Letters to the newspapers denounced the party as a 'disgusting exhibition' and 'immature, vulgar posturing from a class of people who should know better'. One even ranted, 'This is the type of behaviour that leads to Communism.'

Movers and Shakers

In London, the vogue for cocktails was reflected in the more exclusive hotels, such as the Ritz Carlton, where guests could meet for a pre-dinner Manhattan in the American bar.

Barmen became the talk of the town. The Savoy bar boasted Harry Craddock, an American who fled the Prohibition and invented the White Lady cocktail.

Similarly, Harry McElhone from Dundee, a celebrated barman at Ciro's in South Tampa, took over Harry's New York Bar in Paris, after it was dismantled and shipped there by his former boss, Tod Slain.

The cocktail craze even spawned its own ballet, produced by Jonathan Wylie in 1920. *The Passing Show* tour of 1920 kicked off at the Hippodrome, Liverpool in March. Designer Marcelle de St Martin created fabulous costumes for My Lady Liqueur and the sixteen American cocktails that were characters in the show: Clover Club, Bride, Martini, Sloe Gin, Sherry Cobbler, Crème de Menthe, Egg Flip, Pousse Café (a cocktail with layers of colour), Stinger, Manhattan, Rattlesnake, Royal Smile, Crème de Cocoa, Champagne Cocktail, Brain Duster and Infuriator.

Sister Act

Sales of cocktail shakers, cabinets and olive dishes soared throughout the twenties as more and more people threw cocktail parties at home.

In 1922, the world-famous dancing double act the Dolly Sisters returned to New York from London and managed to smuggle a portable mahogany cocktail bar about four feet long with a silver foot-rail, a towel, a drip trough, and a cut-glass dish for cloves, into Prohibition-era America. They took great delight in shaking up exotic concoctions for their many high-society guests.

Drinkie-Poos

While cocktails were frowned upon by many, their fruity and creamy content proved a hit with women and before long the pre-dinner cocktail replaced whisky and sherry as an aperitif in country houses across the land – and even in Buckingham Palace.

The Duchess of York, Lady Elizabeth Bowes-Lyon, was an enthusiastic fan of the drinks if not the word. As 'cocktail' was banned from Royal circles for being 'too American', the fashionable young newly-wed, who was to become the beloved Queen Mum in later life, referred to her mixed aperitifs as 'drinkie-poos'. Her preferred tipples were two large gin and Dubonnets before lunch and a few dry martinis as a pre-dinner drink.

JAZZ IT UP

Jazz transformed nightlife across the Western world, especially in London, Paris and American cities such as New York, Chicago and, of course, New Orleans. But the jazz age was not just about the music – it was the soundtrack to a way of life which included late-night drinking clubs, cocktails, louche living, gambling and, most of all, dancing.

Dance Crazy

In the frenzy of fun that followed the war, the traditional waltz and the foxtrot – classic ballroom dances usually performed 'in hold' – were replaced with the less stuffy moves of the

Shimmy, the Black Bottom and the dance that epitomised the era most of all: the Charleston.

The original dance was developed by African-Americans in the United States in the early part of the twentieth century, and was first seen on the Broadway stage in 1922 and 1923, when the steps appeared in the *Ziegfield Follies* and the Irving C Miller production *Liza*.

The name was coined by composer James P Johnson, who claimed he first heard the beat from dockers in Charleston, South Carolina, and used it in a number — which he called 'Charleston' — for the show *Runnin' Wild*.

Kicking Up a Storm

The Charleston spread like wildfire in the speakeasies of the Prohibition era, as the flappers threw caution to the wind and combined cocktails with kicks. The fact that it was considered immoral by the stuffy middle classes merely added to the delight of these saucy young rebels, who scoffed at the 'drys'.

On Your Marks . . .

Charleston competitions were widespread in America and many famous actresses, including Joan Crawford and Ginger Rogers, used them as a stepping stone to a career in movies. In 1923, a craze for dance marathons swept the US. Promoters offered prizes to contestants who could stay on their feet the longest and it was not unusual for the leading contestants to dance for forty or fifty hours. They literally danced until they dropped.

In her book, *High Times, Hard Times*, former marathon contestant Anita O'Day wrote: 'It seems unbelievable now but there were once 15,000 people – promoters, emcees, floor judges, trainers, nurses, cooks, janitors, cashiers, ticket-takers, publicity agents, promotion men, musicians, contestants and even a lawyer – whose main source of income over a number of years came from endurance shows.'

Dance Lessons

In 1925, the Charleston trend had become so mainstream that, according to a *New York Times* article, white householders were now employing black domestic staff with the condition that they knew the dance and could teach it to their employers.

The fashion hit the UK in the same year, when seventeen-year-old American flapper Louise Brooks – later a famous star of the silent movies – became the first person to dance the Charleston in London while working at the Café de Paris.

Who's That Girl? Louise Brooks

— ★ —

Famous For: After a debut as a bob-haired flapper in the 1925 movie *A Social Celebrity*, she became a style icon and model.

— ★ —

Career Notes: The celebrated actress made twenty more silent movies, including an immoral femme fatale in *Pandora's Box* and a disgraced teen in *Diary of a Lost Girl.* But the advent of 'talkies' led to the end of her career after she walked out on a contract when the studio tried to drop her salary. She then began a new career as a film historian. She died in 1985.

— ★ —

Sound Bite: In *Lulu in Hollywood*, she wrote, 'I have a gift for enraging people, but if I ever bore you it will be with a knife.'

Queen Bee

American dancer Bee Jackson is thought to be the first white girl to have danced the Charleston. Having seen the black cast of *Runnin' Wild* perform it, she asked Lyda Webb, dancer at the Club Alabam, to give her lessons and, in 1924, she danced it on Broadway in *The Silver Slipper*. She then took it on tour with various engagements in New York, California, Paris and London.

Billed as 'the champion shimmy shaker and Charleston dancer from America', the young hoofer was a huge hit in the cabaret at London's Piccadilly Hotel and a favourite at the nearby Kit Cat Club.

It is thought the popular expression 'the bee's knees' is a reference to Miss Jackson's legendary Charleston.

Deadly Dancing

In 1926, the *Oxnard Courier* ran an article denouncing jazz dances as 'dangerous sports' and claiming that, according to one eminent French physician, it was adding 'Charleston knee' to mankind's ills.

In fact, many thought it even more dangerous than that – and they had a point...

◆ On 16 August 1925, the *New York Times* reported that William Franken, a fireman, broke his leg while demonstrating the dance to his colleagues. As a result it was recommended the Charleston be avoided at the upcoming Fireman's Annual Ball.

◆ In the summer of 1926, a group of teenagers drowned after Arthur Tessier, a Charleston champion, demonstrated the dance to five friends on a rowing boat on St Mary's River in Michigan. The boat capsized and all six drowned.

◆ In 1925, tragedy struck in Boston when the local dance venue, the Pickwick Club, collapsed, killing forty-four revellers. The horrific event was blamed on the dancers and *Variety* reported that 'the vibrations of Charleston dancers caused the place to collapse'.

Daredevil Dancers

But of course, disapproval and danger were nothing but enticing to the flappers and gents of the jazz age – if anything, it only made the craze catch on quicker. West Virginian jazz singer Ada 'Bricktop' Smith was partly responsible for its wildfire spread. In 1925, she met Cole Porter in Paris, after he watched her sing one of his songs – 'I'm in Love Again' – in her own club, Le Grand Duc. Afterwards, he asked her if she knew the Charleston, and she confirmed that she had learned it in New York, although at that time it was not yet the fashion in Paris.

According to William McBrien's biography, *Cole Porter*, the composer then told her, 'I'm going to give Charleston cocktail parties at my house two or three times a week, and you're going to teach everyone to dance the Charleston.'

Bricktop duly complied, and found herself at the Porters' elegant Parisian home instructing fifty of Cole's friends, including the Aga Khan and the celebrated American gossip columnist Elsa Maxwell, in the intricacies of the new dance craze. As Bricktop put it, 'I was the dance teacher to the most elegant members of the international set.'

The Jazz Movement

And the world's love of jazz truly had gone international. For the new dance crazes, such as the iconic Charleston, would have been nothing without the music that got toes tapping and knees knocking with such irresistible rhythm. Played by black musicians since the turn of the twentieth century, jazz music originated in the southern states of America. It first became popular in the bars and clubs of New Orleans, and that city later became the very centre of the jazz movement.

Through the migration of southern musicians like Jelly Roll Morton, Louis Armstrong and Duke Ellington (who was considered the most influential player in bringing jazz to the mainstream), the jazz movement quickly spread from New Orleans to New York, and there became part of the Harlem Renaissance, an explosion of negro literature, art and music, which soon caught the attention of white writers and composers – and ultimately led to the runaway popularity of jazz amongst the trendsetters of the day. By the mid-twenties, the use of 'negro bands' in clubs and private parties was all the rage.

Speak Easy

'New Orleans had a great tradition of celebration. Opera, military marching bands, folk music, the blues, different types of church music, ragtime, echoes of traditional African drumming, and all of the dance styles that went with this music could be heard and seen throughout the city. When all of these kinds of music blended into one, jazz was born.'

Jazz musician and historian Wynton Marsalis in the curriculum of New York's Lincoln Center

Who's That Boy? Duke Ellington

— ⭑ —

Famous For: Spreading the popularity of jazz music and elevating it to an art form. He also composed over a thousand songs in a career that spanned more than fifty years.

— ⭑ —

Career Notes: Born Edward Kennedy Ellington in Washington, he moved to Harlem, the hub of the jazz revolution, in the early twenties. In 1923, his seven-piece band, Elmer Snowdon, became resident band at the Hollywood Club and Duke took over as band leader a year later. He went on to a residency at Harlem's famous Cotton Club and a lucrative broadcasting career. He also recorded hundreds of hit records, including 'It Don't Mean a Thing (If It Ain't Got That Swing)'.

— ⭑ —

Sound Bite: In his book *The Swing Era*, musician Gunther Shuler wrote: 'Music was indeed his mistress; it was his total life and his commitment to it was incomparable and unalterable. In jazz he was a giant among giants. And in twentieth-century music, he may yet one day be recognised as one of the half-dozen greatest masters of our time.'

A Chorus of Disapproval

Not everyone was jazzing it up in the Roaring Twenties. While the Bright Young Things were dancing the night away, there was a flood of disapproval from all walks of society who feared the 'negro music' and racy dancing were corrupting their youth. The *Daily Mail* denounced the Charleston as 'reminiscent only of negro orgies'.

Women's magazines published frequent articles about the evils of jazz and in December 1921 the *Ladies' Home Journal* printed a piece by John R McMahon, in which dance professional Fenton D claimed that 'jazz is worse than the saloon'.

He continued: 'Those moaning saxophones and the rest of the instruments with their broken, jerky rhythm make a purely sensual appeal. They call out to the low and rowdy instinct. All of us dancing teachers know this to be a fact. We have seen the effect of jazz music on our young pupils. It makes them act in a restless and rowdy manner.'

On the Record

White musicians The Original Dixieland Jazz Band were the first to record 'The Sound of New Orleans'. Until 1922, record companies shied away from putting African-American artists on vinyl. Vaudeville star Mamie Smith became the first African-American to make a commercial record, when she recorded 'Crazy Blues' and 'It's Right Here for You' with the Okeh Record Company in 1920.

The success of the records led to many more companies, such as Columbia and Paramount, seeking out black jazz artists.

Classic releases of the decade include Jelly Roll Morton and his Hot Red Peppers recordings from 1926 to 1928 and Louis Armstrong's Hot Five and Hot Seven recordings from 1925 to 1928.

Speak Easy

'Jazz originally was the accompaniment of the voodoo dancer, stimulating the half-crazed barbarian to the vilest deeds. The weird chant, accompanied by the syncopated rhythm of the voodoo invokers, has also been employed by other barbaric people to stimulate brutality and sensuality. That it has a demoralising effect upon the human brain has been demonstrated by many scientists ... Jazz disorganises all regular laws and order; it stimulates to extreme deeds, to a breaking away from all rules and conventions; it is harmful and dangerous, and its influence is wholly bad.'

Extract from the article 'Does Jazz Put the Sin in Syncopation?' by Anne Shaw Faulkner, head of the Music Department of the General Federation of Women's Clubs, published in *Ladies' Home Journal*, August 1921

Bessie Smith, dubbed the Empress of the Blues, made her first record in 1923. 'Downhearted Blues' sold 780,000 copies. Frank Walker was working for Columbia Records when she came into the studio. 'She looked anything but a singer … tall and fat and scared to death,' he said in Lucy Moore's *Anything Goes*, but added that when she began to sing, 'I had never heard anything like the torture and torment she put into the music of her people. It was the blues, and she meant it.'

Top-Ten Hits of the Twenties

1. Al Jolson, 'Swanee' (1920)
2. Paul Whiteman, 'Whispering' (1920)
3. Vernon Dalhart, 'The Prisoner's Song' (1925)
4. Isham Jones, 'It Had to Be You' (1924)
5. Bessie Smith, 'Downhearted Blues' (1923)
6. Al Jolson, 'California, Here I Come' (1924)
7. Gene Austin, 'Bye Bye, Blackbird' (1926)
8. Ben Bernie, 'Sweet Georgia Brown' (1925)
9. George Gershwin, 'Rhapsody in Blue' (1924)
10. Eddie Cantor, 'Makin' Whoopee' (1929)

Who's That Boy? Louis Armstrong

— ★ —

Famous For: Playing trumpet and singing on some of the biggest hits of the jazz age and beyond.

— ★ —

Career Notes: Born in 1901, in Louisiana, Louis moved to Chicago at the age of twenty-one to join Joe 'King' Oliver's Creole Jazz Band and later joined the highly respected Fletcher Henderson Orchestra in New York. From 1924 he recorded with contemporary jazz singers including Bessie Smith, Ma Rainey and Alberta Hunter. In 1925, he formed his own group, Louis Armstrong and the Hot Five (sometimes the Hot Seven) and their 1928 recording of 'West End Blues', including a legendary trumpet intro from Louis, is considered a masterpiece of the jazz age. He soon moved into vocal and his version of 'Ain't Misbehavin'' was one of the biggest hits of the decade.

— ★ —

Sound Bite: Asked to define jazz, Louis reportedly answered, 'If you have to ask what jazz is, you'll never know.'

Sex, Drugs and Jazz

Notorious gangster Al Capone, who ran the speakeasy scene in Prohibition-era Chicago, was a huge jazz fan. Under his patronage the new sound flourished in the city and the greats of the era, including Bessie Smith, Louis Armstrong and Duke Ellington, could often be heard in his clubs as Capone himself clapped from the audience.

One night in 1926, Fats Waller's set was interrupted by gun-wielding gangsters who bundled him into a car and drove him to the Hawthorne Inn in Cicero, where Capone was throwing a party. For three days party-goers drank champagne, romped with showgirls and snorted cocaine before the celebrated pianist was driven home, loaded with cash from a grateful Capone.

By the mid-twenties Chicago boasted 10,000 clubs and bars where music was played, while New York had 500 dance halls and 800 cabarets.

London (Night)Life

As America banned the booze, London celebrated the end of the Great War in style. In 1921, the wartime Licensing Act was finally altered to allow drink to be served until 12.30 a.m., as long as it was accompanied by food. When the cocktail parties at swish Mayfair houses got 'too tired-making' the Bright Young People headed to their favourite London nightclubs, which usually began filling up around 11.30 p.m. There the restless young souls could round off the evening doing the Charleston, Shimmy and Heebie-Jeebie to the thrilling sounds of the house jazz band.

The Places to Be

◆ At the Trocadero, a 25-guinea clothes voucher could be won for the best-dressed lady in the room. The prize – which equates to just over £900 today – was awarded by Paris designer Monsieur Paul Poiret, who was enjoying an extended stay in the UK to 'study, criticise and suggest'.

◆ The Kit Cat Club, in Haymarket, was the first nightclub to open in a purpose-built venue and at least thirty sons of the nobility were on the members' list.

◆ At the Café de Paris, the dashing Prince of Wales could often be found on the dance floor.

◆ At the Embassy Club, run by the well-connected restauranteur Luigi Naintré, guests were seated in accordance with their social standing and the dance floor was packed with bodies shimmying away to the music of bandleader Bert Ambrose, the most celebrated in London.

Who's That Boy? Bert Ambrose

— ★ —

Famous For: Packing the Embassy Club every night through most of the twenties, as well as recording his songs for various record companies.

— ★ —

Career Notes: Born in the East End, the son of a Jewish wool merchant, he learned to play the violin as a child and, after moving to the United States with his aunt as a teenager, he began playing professionally. At the age of twenty, he was asked to form a fifteen-piece band at New York Palais Royale and six years later, he moved back to the UK and formed a seven-piece band at the Embassy Club. Offered a better job in New York, he left two years later, prompting pleading messages from his ex-employer to return. He was finally persuaded by a cable from the Prince of Wales himself, which read: 'The Embassy needs you. Come back — Edward.'

— ★ —

Sound Bite: Loelia Ponsonby was a regular at the Embassy and recalled: 'Ambrose and his band played – the best dance band in London, we considered. Ambitious hostesses tried to lure him away to play at their dances but he was hard to capture.'

Rebellious Youth

Loelia Ponsonby's parents attempted to ban her from nightclubs, as they considered all such venues 'equally reprehensible', and sure to give a girl a 'bad name'. But they failed to deter their spirited daughter.

'Of course I went to the Embassy whenever I got the chance,' she wrote. 'Only an angel would have stayed away. It was the favourite meeting place of all my friends and so it was like having a lovely party where one knew everyone.'

Night Owls

The nightlife of London, of course, catered for all tastes – from the respectable venues frequented by Loelia and her ilk to the illegal basement bars and dance clubs with their after-hours drinking and dancing girls. Unlike the young upper-class denizens of the dance halls, Loelia's parents 'did not see the difference between a place like Uncle's where you drank beer in a teacup in case the police called, or the Fifty-Three [*sic*] with its squad of girls, and Ciro's and the Embassy which had nothing sinister about them'.

But while the well-behaved daughters of dukes and lords might stick to the more respectable venues, the Bright Young People couldn't resist the lure of the seedier establishments, where all walks of life rubbed shoulders on the dance floor. The Blue Lantern at Ham Yard was a favourite hangout for artists and intellectuals, such as Anthony Powell and Tallulah Bankhead, as was the Cave of Harmonies, in Charlotte Street.

After Hours

At the 43 Club, a Gerrard Street haunt run by the notorious hostess Kate Meyrick, you could savour a tipple long after the legal closing time – at a heavy price. By her own admission, she added over a third to the price after hours. Below are her own costings for champagne and beer, detailed in her book *Secrets of the 43 Club*.

	Price in 1923	*Today's equivalent*
Champagne, bottle		
Cost price	12s 6d	£27.80
Sale price	22s 6d–30s	£50–£67
After-hours price	30s–£2	£67–£89
Beer, bottle		
Cost price	4½d	83p
Sale price	8d	£1.48
After-hours price	1s 6d	£3.34

Nightclub Nibbles

Evening food was restricted to sandwiches and, as many of the illustrious patrons had already been to dinner or to parties, was really only a concession to the law. The only money-spinner when it came to food was breakfast – served to the many revellers who stayed until the early hours.

Food Prices	*Price in 1923*	*Today's equivalent*
Sandwiches	£2s 6d	£5.56
Kippers, bread and butter and coffee	£3s 6d	£7.78
Eggs and bacon, bread and butter and coffee	£3s 6d	£7.78

Who's That Girl? Kate 'Ma' Meyrick

— ★ —

Famous For: The most notorious nightclub owner of the 1920s.

— ★ —

Career Notes: The mother of eight left her doctor husband in 1919 after fifteen years of marriage and in 1921 opened the 43 Club in Gerrard Street as a way of funding her children's education. By her own reckoning, around £500,000 passed through her many clubs – the equivalent of £23.7 million today. A string of raids by police shut her down and put her in prison time after time, but with her daughters' help she reopened for trade on each occasion and expanded her empire, with more clubs in London and one in Paris. Despite the fortune the clubs made over her lifetime, when she passed away in January 1933 she had just £58 (£2,750 in today's money) to her name.

— ★ —

Sound Bite: After one of her many arrests, Mrs Meyrick emerged from the police station with the words, 'The police are always so kind to me.'

Making Merry with Meyrick

Kate Meyrick became a celebrity in London circles — before becoming infamous for her many arrests and spells in jail.

On a typical evening at the 43 you could find foreign royalty, such as the King of Sweden, sharing the dance floor with stars like Tallulah Bankhead, various peers of the realm and theatre impresario Jimmy White, as well as the occasional London gangster or murderer.

Mrs Meyrick herself became very well connected; two of her daughters married members of the peerage, while a third would go on to marry a lord.

In Evelyn Waugh's most famous novel, *Brideshead Revisited*, Sebastian, Charles and a friend visit a club at 100 Sink Street, a thinly veiled reference to 43 Gerrard Street. Mrs Meyrick becomes 'Mrs Mayfield' in the book.

Speak Easy

'I say, do any of you ever go to the Forty-Three?'

From *Afternoon Men* by Anthony Powell

Killjoy

All this gay abandon and wild living soon came to the attention of the Home Office and, in particular, a rather joyless Home Secretary called Lord William Joynson-Hicks – christened 'The Gay Lord Jix' by *Punch* – who was appointed in 1924. As far as he was concerned, every supper club, nightclub and dance hall was a den of iniquity and immoral behaviour.

He began a series of late-night police raids and was shocked to find figures from his own aristocratic set featuring on the members' list. During the very first raid of the 43, Mrs Meyrick's distinguished guests found themselves in front of Bow Street magistrates and fined forty shillings each.

Far from frightening the Bright Young People, the raids were considered 'too thrilling' and the newspaper reports gave them a new notoriety, making them the celebrities of the day.

One raid on the Kit Cat Club came the night after the Prince of Wales had danced there, and in another, Elizabeth Ponsonby was forced to eat a piece of sausage which had been sitting about for quite some time, in order to comply with the 1921 licensing law.

Speak Easy

'At the station we were kept waiting for what seemed like weary hours while the police verified the names and addresses which had been given them. All the young people in our luckless party were so kind to me during that time. Not a word of reproach for my having landed them in this trying situation, not even the expression of a single regret. Instead they beguiled the time away and cheered one another up with popular songs.'

Kate Meyrick remembers a raid on
the 43 in *Secrets of the 43 Club*

The Gargoyle Club

The Bright Young People, as ever, weren't averse to making their own fun when it came to the dashing nightclub scene. When he wanted somewhere new to dance with his girlfriend, David Tennant, the son of Lord Glenconner and one of the leading members of the Bright Young People, took matters into his own hands and opened the Gargoyle Club in Dean Street. The venue promised a fashionable dance venue with an artistic bent, where 'struggling writers, painters, poets and musicians will be offered the best food and wine at prices they can afford'. Somerset Maugham was among its patrons as were various members of the Guinness and Rothschild families.

On the advice of his friend, Henry Matisse, David lined the walls with shards of broken mirrors and hung the artist's paintings. Membership was seven guineas (£345 today) but free to the 'deserving artistic poor' as the atmosphere was decidedly bohemian. Daphne Fielding remarked that 'the Gargoyle seemed to transform ordinary conventional people into bohemians; on becoming members they even began to dress quite differently'.

The Lovely Lido

In France, the place to be was undoubtedly the decadent Lido on the Champs Élysées, at the heart of elegant Paris. A heady mixture of a swimming pool, restaurant, cabaret and club, it was inspired by the success of the Venetian Lido and billed as the most luxurious venue in all of Europe. It opened on 18 February 1928 amid a fanfare of hyperbole – but it lived up to its promise.

A block long, the Lido was entered via elevator, which descended to the basement to what revellers described as a 'magical underworld'. Here the pink-and-blue marbled pool took centre stage, with a lavish bar at one end, grand marble pillars surrounding its edge, and multi-coloured lights setting a dreamy scene. The pool's water was lightly scented with hyacinth.

The ballroom of the Lido, meanwhile, boasted a glass floor which was illuminated from beneath by red lights, as well as impressive scarlet drapes tied with gold tassels. The walls throughout the huge building were adorned with stunning paintings in the Venetian style, and party-goers could choose from a tearoom, ballroom, restaurant or bar for their high jinks and cocktails.

The fabulously named nightspot The Frolics, at 30 Rue de Gramont, attracted the smart international society set. Described by the *Dancing Times* as 'the most chic location in Paris', it offered late-night suppers, gambling, drinking, dancing, and music by the Red Devils Jazz Band.

Puttin' on the Ritz

The Ritz bar in Paris was one venue where the great and the glittering could always be found. A favourite haunt of Cole Porter and Noël Coward – who named a play after the bar which never saw the light of day – the venue was split into two, with a men-only bar and a mixed bar.

In *The Sweet and Twenties*, Beverley Nichols wrote, 'I adored the Ritz Bar. Think of it ... champagne cocktails at a bob apiece! And the scent of Gauloise cigarettes, and the echo of Madame Chanel's laughter ... and the sudden flurry of [cabaret star] Mistinguette, wrapped to the hilt in monkey fur, stepping over the sacred masculine threshold in pursuit of her latest young man, who is drinking behind a pillar with a rather dubious Jamaican.'

DUKES AND DEBUTANTES

My second debutante year. If the first year went by without an engagement, we were given a second chance ... It was OK to dance with a stranger who had bowed and asked you ... You flirted with your eyes, with jokes while dancing, accepting if he wished to do nice little things for you. Only a girl engaged to be married could take an unchaperoned walk ... Kissing was a real no-no and a stolen pleasure.

Marie Therese Miller-Degenfeld, *Memoirs*

The 'smart set' of the Roaring Twenties may have included a high percentage of wealthy and titled youngsters, but a great many more were found in the ballrooms rather than the basement clubs. In Britain, the weekend parties at country houses continued much as they had before the war and the London season, with its debutante balls and afternoon soirees, saw the more conventional young toffs on their best behaviour.

The Other Half

In *Grace and Favour*, Loelia Ponsonby wrote that the twenties 'have sometimes been called the Night-club age. Well, they were and they weren't. The majority of the inhabitants of London never saw the inside of a nightclub and wouldn't have known in which street to look for one. On the other hand you couldn't help hearing them talked about. They were a novelty and they were news. Bishops denounced them. Old ladies deplored them. The dowdier debutantes envied the more dashing ones who boasted that they had slipped away from the ball while their mother was at supper and had "a marvellous-time-my-dear at a *frightfully* low haunt".'

Courting Favour

Despite the high profile of the Bright Young People, not everyone in the 1920s was throwing out the old traditions and delighting in subverting the status quo. For many of the well-to-do, life continued in the same vein it always had. Every year, another swathe of society youngsters entered the courting scene to be paired off with a suitable suitor, as the aristocracy sought to match-make in their time-honoured tradition.

Coming Out

For the young lady of the aristocracy, adulthood began at seventeen, when she was presented at Buckingham Palace, along with all the other debutantes (debs) of the season, for a 'coming out ceremony'. At Queen Charlotte's Ball, the teenagers – some spirited and giggly, some terrified into silence – filed past King George V and Queen Mary wearing ostrich feather headdresses and virginal white dresses with long trains. This was the highlight of the debutante season, where young ladies of impeccable breeding were presented to eligible bachelors, known as 'debs' delights'. The aim was to find a suitable husband by the end of the season.

Queen Charlotte's Ball, where the debutantes were presented to the King and Queen, was started in 1780 by King George III to celebrate his wife's birthday. A lasting feature of the event was an eight-foot white cake, similar to a wedding cake, which became the centrepiece of the ballroom.

Dowdy Debs

For Mary Pakenham, daughter of Lord Longford, the deb season was excruciatingly dull and the debs even duller.

In her book *Brought Up and Brought Out*, she wrote: 'In my day all the debutantes were dowdy unless they wanted to be branded as unpresentably fast, but the actual year that I came out was a bumper dowdy year.'

She complained that the life of a debutante, far from being a glamorous round of gaiety, meant monotonous lunches and endless portions of the fashionable dish du jour – in her case, grapefruit. 'Soon there is nobody left but yourself and two monstrously ugly girls. Your hostess catches sight of you three and looks quickly away.'

Speak Easy

'They were practically deformed. Some were without chins. Some had no foreheads. Hardly any of them had backs to their heads.'

Lady Mary Pakenham scathingly reviews the 'debs' delights', *Brought Up and Brought Out*

Social Butterfly

Loelia Ponsonby came out in the early 1920s and found that, after a childhood of wearing old clothes and having no contact with boys: 'Suddenly I was supposed to break from my chrysalis, a gorgeous mature butterfly, endowed with complete savoir faire, with every social art and grace, conversationally adept, and so physically attractive that dozens of completely strange men would immediately queue up to ask me, if not for my hand, at least to dance.'

The London season could mean as many as four balls a week, and that meant a lot of late nights. After hours of dancing, supper was served until midnight. It usually consisted of a clear soup, some cold meats and game, often quail, and potatoes.

Belle of the Ball

Nina Ogilvie-Grant, Countess of Seafield was the most sought-after debutante of the twenties. Tiny, auburn-haired and blue-eyed, the young beauty inherited her title, and Cullen Castle in Banffshire, Scotland, at the age of nine. Her two estates netted her an annual income of some £750,000 (£33.4 million today) and she was set to inherit a further £19 million (£845 million) when her grandmother passed away.

On 'coming out' she naturally became, according to the *Evening Independent* in 1925, 'the most important debutante in Europe':

She is petted, feted, flattered, and wooed from one end of the United Kingdom to the other; she is the recipient of a perfect avalanche of invitations bidding her to receptions, house parties, balls and teas. Magnificent bouquets are showered on her bearing the cards of society's pet beaux. Aristocratic British dowagers with marriageable sons are distinctly on her trail; in fact it is said on the best of authority, that two queens are among the mammas who would like to see the pretty little Countess of Seafield enter their respective families.

Despite overtures from the Romanian royal family, Nina eventually eloped with Derek Studley-Herbert, a member of a minor aristocratic family.

Nancy Mitford recalled a weekend stay at Cullen Castle, home of the coveted Nina, in 1927: 'We haven't once been to bed before 2. Pyjama parties every night in Nina's sitting room, which is like a gala night at the Florida.' On another occasion, quoted in *Nancy Mitford* by Selena Hastings, she wrote to brother Tom that she was 'very drunk on one of Nina's cocktails'.

Weekend Haunts

Despite the allure of the London season, the Bright Young People and their more sober counterparts often left the hustle and bustle of the big city for their favourite country retreats, where the fun would continue. The Mitfords' homes in Oxfordshire, first Asthall Manor and later Swinbrook House, were favourite weekend haunts, and in a biography of Diana Mosley by Jan Dalley, Jessica Mitford recalled the large groups of friends she and her sisters inflicted on their parents, Lord and Lady Redesdale: 'At weekends they would swoop down from Oxford and London in their merry hordes to be greeted with solid disapproval from my mother and furious glares from my father.'

Other favoured homes included Schulbrede Priory, the Sussex home of Elizabeth Ponsonby's family; Farringdon, the home of Lord Berners; and the country pile near Ascot which was home to the Jungman sisters' mother and stepfather, Beatrice and Richard Guinness.

Who's That Girl? Nancy Mitford

— ★ —

Famous For: Bestselling novels including *Love in a Cold Climate,* as well as for being one of the celebrated Mitford sisters.

— ★ —

Career Notes: Born in Belgravia and brought up at Asthall Manor, she was the eldest of six daughters of Baron Redesdale, the celebrated Mitford sisters. Although less of an entrenched member of the Bright Young People than her little sister Diana, she numbered many of them among her friends and attended frequent weekend parties with them. She had a long-term relationship with Hamish Erskine, who was actually homosexual, before eventually marrying Peter Rodd.

— ★ —

Sound Bite: Brian Howard told Harold Acton she was: 'A delicious creature, quite pyrotechnical my dear, and sometimes even profound, and would you believe it she's hidden among the cabbages of the Cotswolds?'

Speak Easy

'I am normal, my wife is normal but my daughters are each more foolish than the other!'

Lord Redesdale, father to the Mitford sisters, quoted in *The Mitford Girls* by Mary S Lovell

Country Capers

The rowdy bawdiness of the Mayfair parties gave way to more innocent high jinks in the respectable stately homes of Britain. The young debutantes may have been proficient at teasing and flirting, but bed-hopping was out of the question for the majority.

Barbara Cartland remembered, 'In country houses there was a lot of ragging ... In the twenties I was always prepared for an apple pie bed with a bunch of holly at the foot, or pillows covered with flour ... Like the other girls, I found it great fun to tease the men until they pursued me with a soda-syphon, or to sew up the bottoms of a man's pyjama legs as we imagined him taking hours to unpick them before he could get into bed. It never crossed my mind that he might sleep without them.'

Social Climbers

The rigid nature of Edwardian society, which put a heavy emphasis on background and breeding, had let down its barriers during the war years and by the twenties, a few determined social climbers had made their mark on society. The well-polished mantelpieces of the upper classes were adorned with treasured invitations to lunches and soirées thrown by hostesses whose humble beginnings would once have made them socially unacceptable. Mrs Ronnie Greville, whose summons to her palatial Surrey home Polesden Lacey were much sought after, was the illegitimate daughter of a brewer, while Lady Cunard, who was married to the heir of a shipping line, was the American granddaughter of an Irish rebel who had changed her name from Maud to Emerald to give it a grander ring.

Despite their inherently snobbish chatter, the Bright Young People gave talented artists and writers the chance to climb up the social ladder and no one benefited more than Cecil Beaton, who would become a celebrated society photographer, and novelist Evelyn Waugh. On marrying into the aristocratic family of his first wife Evelyn Gardner, the daughter of Lord and Lady Burghclere, Waugh remarked that his mother-in-law was 'quite inexpressibly pained' by her daughter's lowly choice.

Hostess with the Mostest

Regardless of this more permissive age, however, the battle for social superiority was still being waged in drawing rooms and ballrooms up and down the country, as one hostess pitted her skills and connections against the other. While their backgrounds would once have made them less than desirable company, two formidable ladies stood out from the crowd: the aforementioned Mrs Ronald Greville and her valiant social sparring partner, Lady Emerald Cunard.

Speak Easy

'The hostesses of the twenties were like great galleons, sailing the social seas with all flags flying and all guns manned, relentlessly pursuing their charted course – and not above indulging in a little piracy if the occasion demanded it.'

From *The Sweet and Twenties* by Beverley Nichols

Mrs Greville

Mrs Greville, called Maggie by her close friends, was a widowed socialite whose vast fortune came from her father John McEwan's Scottish brewing business. According to Beverley Nichols, she was proud of her humble background and would say, 'I'd rather be a beeress than a peeress.' But she counted Queen Mary and the Duke and Duchess of York among her closest friends, and even lent the young couple her Surrey home for their honeymoon in 1923. In fact, she was so used to entertaining royalty from around the world that she was once heard to complain, while waiting for the Queen of Spain to arrive for dinner at her London home in Charles Street, 'One uses up *so* many red carpets in a season.'

Her magnificent spreads at her tea parties were all brought in by Bowles the butler, and are here fondly recalled by former guest Beverley Nichols: 'Maggie's teas were terrific, with great Georgia teapots, and Indian *or* China, and muffins and cream cakes and silver kettles sending up their steam, and Queen Mary saying, "Indian, if you please, and no sugar."'

Lady Cunard

Lady Emerald Cunard, meanwhile, was an American socialite who had married into a great deal of money, as husband Sir Bache Cunard was the grandson of the founder of the famous shipping line. Her own royal connections extended only to the party-loving Prince of Wales, but her huge home at the corner of Grosvenor Square was constantly humming with the likes of Somerset Maugham, composer Sir Thomas Beecham, writers Beverley Nichols and George Moore (who was in love with her), and the leading politicians of the day.

In *Sir Thomas Beecham – A Centenary Tribute*, biographer Alan Jefferson wrote, 'Her salon became the most important Mecca for musicians, painters, sculptors, poets and writers as well as for politicians, soldiers, aristocrats – indeed anybody so long as they were interesting.' Her 1948 obituary in *The Times* called her: 'The most lavish hostess of her day.'

Speak Easy

'Red carpets were reserved for Royals. There were enchanted nights in the twenties when the people around Grosvenor Square were giving so many grand parties that the pavements were as bright as a sunset.'

From *The Sweet and Twenties* by Beverley Nichols

Last Hurrah

Yet the pomp and finery of society parties often hid the painful reality – the aristocracy was undoubtedly in decline, in both wealth and influence. The huge country piles which were filled with laughter and the clinking of glasses at weekends were a massive financial drain, which could no longer be ignored. Land values had crashed and death duties had swiped many an inherited fortune, leaving families unable to pay for the upkeep of their palatial homes.

Many carved out a new life in colonial destinations or moved to Paris, where the cost of living was cheaper, as the Earl of Glasgow did. Those young men who had survived the war looked to new money when it came to marriage, wedding the daughters of American business magnates, or rich widows, a tradition which had become the norm over some thirty years.

It is estimated that around a hundred American women married into the titled ranks of Britain between 1880 and 1920. The drawing rooms of country houses and Mayfair mansions were now the domain of the American society hostess, like Nancy Astor and Lady Cunard.

To the Auction House

Those who could not increase wealth through marriage were often forced to sell land and other properties, such as artwork. In 1926, for example, the Duke of Athol was forced to sell land worth £114,000 (over £5 million today). Two years later he sold another £200,000 worth (£9.4 million) as well as the Duchess's emerald tiara, which sold for £6,500 (£305,000 today) and two pearl necklaces worth £7,200 and £5,500 (£338,000 and £258,000 today). But four years later he was still struggling with a total debt of £380,000 – the equivalent of £20 million.

Speak Easy

'The stately homes of England,
We proudly represent.
We only keep them up
For Americans to rent.'

From 'The Stately Homes of England' by Noël Coward

Going Out in Style

Nevertheless, the impending financial misery of the upper classes didn't prevent some families from putting on a show for guests. Duff Cooper noted, after a visit to the Duke of Marlborough's family seat, Blenheim Castle, that 'the Duke keeps high state – wears his garter for dinner and has a host of powdered footmen'.

Barbara Cartland also recalled: 'At Trent Park, the country home of the enigmatic Sir Philip Sassoon, guests were supplied with every published newspaper when they were called in the morning and, at night, when the men went up to dress for dinner, there was a cocktail and the choice of a red carnation or gardenia buttonhole waiting for them in their bedrooms.'

UPSTAIRS, DOWNSTAIRS

Domestic servants are more loyal by nature than politicians.

Sir Richard Bellamy, as played by David Langton, in *Upstairs, Downstairs*

L ife may have been a constant round of cocktails and parties for the lucky few in the 1920s, but for others, the end of the war signalled the resurgence of the daily grind. Huge unemployment (more than 2 million people out of work) in the 1920s meant that a return to life 'below stairs' became a necessity for many men and women: they were lucky to have a job at all.

Between 1921 and 1931 the number of women in service, in England and Wales, rose from 1.1 million to 1.3 million, and the same period saw a rise in male servants from 61,006 to 78,489.

But things weren't what they used to be in the stately homes of Britain and, while the old class system looked like it was still firmly in place, a quiet revolution was stirring in the basement kitchens of the baronial halls ...

Master and Servant

The First World War, coupled with the women's liberation movement and a huge take up of 'the dole', introduced in 1911, had brought a shift in attitudes which irrevocably altered the relationship between master and servant. Gone were the days of unquestioning servitude. Equality on the battlefield meant that many a batman entering the service of his demobbed officers now resented the inequalities of civilian life, and women who had previously been happy to work long hours for little pay now demanded time off and higher wages.

In his memoir *From Hallboy to House Steward*, former butler William Lanceley, who spent forty-three years of his life in service, explained that the jobs that many had taken during the war had opened their eyes to life outside of service. 'It was a novelty to them, the pay was big and they had short hours; hundreds being spoilt for service through it. It made those who returned to service unsettled.'

The Servant Problem

The 1918 Education Act, which made schooling compulsory until the age of fourteen, led to fewer youngsters taking up live-in positions, while a decrease in the average age of newly-weds meant a further fall in the number of single, young ladies who had previously provided a wealth of potential servants.

With the war having emphasised the precious nature of life, people were taking their opportunities where they found them, whether for advancement or for love.

But this new attitude had far-reaching consequences. In smaller homes, the live-in maid now began to be replaced with a 'day girl' or a charwoman. Employment exchanges found themselves inundated with applications for these roles, rather than the residential positions. A *Times* article in 1919 reported that ten applicants came forward for each charwoman job and eight for each day servant's position, while only two women applied for every three residential places.

The problem was so acute that meetings began to be arranged in town halls up and down the country, so that mistresses and potential maids could decide on fair working conditions. In Bromley, for example, maids were to be offered one half-day and evening off each week – plus a half-day on Sunday, a full day once a month and paid annual leave.

The accounts from Stalwell Social Club, in County Durham, show the huge hike in wages for charwomen and other staff from the pre-war period to the twenties. In 1914, the steward received £2 7s (£176 in today's terms), the charwoman ten shillings (£37.40) per week. By 1926, the steward's wages had risen to £6 0s (£272) while the charwoman received £1 5s (£56.60) – a rise of 55 and 51 per cent respectively. In fact, with a cumulative inflation between these years of 89 per cent, that was a reasonable increase, but it all added to soaring household expenditure.

A Fair Deal

As wages for domestics rose in the post-war period, a sub-committee of the Women's Advisory Committee published a suggested pay scale for domestics and dailies. Below are some of the weekly wages considered fair for the time:

Position	Weekly wage	Today's equivalent
Housekeeper	£1 2s 6d	£35
Cook with kitchen and scullery maids	£1 2s 6d	£35
Cook with kitchen maid	19s 6d	£30.50
Kitchen maid	10s	£15.70
Scullery maid	7s 6d	£11.70
Between maid	7s 6d	£11.70
Head housemaid	15s	£23.50
Second housemaid	12s 6d	£19.60
Head nurse	£1	£31.30
Lady's maid	£1	£31.30
Head laundry maid	18s	£28.20
Daily maid	Minimum 9d per hour	£1.17

Servants' Stockings

A maid from Yorkshire told the Ambleside Oral History project she was earning £20 (£948 today) a year, plus £1 (£47.40) for an annual trip home. Her wages had to buy clothes, and these included 'a nice coat for about £2 (£94.80) or a pair of shoes for 12/6d (£29.90)', plus the essential woollen stockings. 'You did an awful lot of kneeling, and you darned and darned the knees until you really couldn't darn them any more, then you had to spend your precious money on a pair of stockings for working.'

Cap and Apron

The revolution in below-stairs working conditions wasn't just limited to holidays and pay. In Harrogate, negotiations not only secured an agreement to a maximum working day of ten hours, but the wearing of the cap was also to become optional for all maids. This seemingly small concession was hugely significant to domestic servants, who saw the traditional headwear as a mark of servitude.

Jean Rennie, whose family's poverty forced her to take up a position as third housemaid in a country house in Argyllshire in 1924, confessed in *Every Other Sunday* that on her appointment 'my greatest horror was the knowledge that I would now have to submit to the badge of servitude – a cap and apron'.

Speak Easy

'I hated that cap until I got to be a cook, and I never wore a cap then. I had a battle royal with one woman I worked for over it, but I'd never wear a cap as a cook.'

Margaret Powell, who became a kitchen maid in 1922, recalls her hatred of the house-maid's cap in her memoirs *Below Stairs*

Changing Times

Margaret Powell entered service in the Hove home of a Reverend Clydesdale and his wife at the age of fifteen. She remembers being appalled that her mother, who had detested her own life 'below stairs', would force her into domestic service. But the twenty-five years that had passed since the older woman's employment had brought considerable change.

'[Mum] forgot the tales she used to tell us – how she went into service when she was fourteen years old in 1895, and how she had to work like a galley slave; an object of derision to the other servants,' wrote Margaret. 'So when I reminded Mum of all this: "Ah," she said, "life is different in service now; the work's not so hard, you get more free time, and the outings and money are better."'

And in fact, the truth was that Mum knew best. Not only were conditions improving for servants, but a more deep-seated change was taking place: the servant-master relationship was evolving in a wholly unprecedented direction.

Power Shift

The shortage of full-time domestic staff meant that, once employed, they were hard to hold on to. The era of the loyal family servant was waning and servants switched houses as often as twice a year, in search of better pay and conditions.

The transient nature of the maids even upset social reformer Violet Markham, who devoted a large part of her life to training 100,000 women for domestic service. In a letter she sent to a friend she complained about the quality of maids in her own London home, writing, 'My path has been so encumbered by odious servant worries and a procession of damsels through the house who arrive with wonderful testimonials and reveal the standard of a lodging house.'

Domestic Duties

Lavinia Swainbank went into service in 1922. She detailed her daily duties in John Burnett's *Useful Toil*:

6.30 a.m.   Rise. Clean grate and lay fire in the Dining Room. Sweep carpet and dust. Clean grate and lay fire in Library. Sweep and dust. Clean grate and lay fire in Drawing Room. Polish floor. Clean grate and lay fire in Morning Room. Sweep and dust Vestibule. Sweep and dust Blue Staircase. All that before ...

8 a.m.   Breakfast in the Servants' Hall.

9 a.m.   Start bedrooms. Help with Bedmaking and slops and fill ewers and carafes. Clean grates and lay fires. Fill up coal boxes and wood baskets. Sweep and dust bedrooms. Clean bathrooms. Change into afternoon uniform.

1 p.m.   Lunch in the Servants' Hall.

Afternoons: clean silver, brass, water cans, trim lamps.

4 p.m.   Tea in the Servants' Hall.

5 p.m.   Light fires in bedrooms.

6 p.m.   Cans of hot water to bedrooms.

7.30 p.m.   Turn down bed, make up fires and empty slops. Fill up coal and wood containers. Leave morning trays set out.

Speak Easy

'The woman in the kitchen has made up her mind to leave tomorrow at only a week's notice – quite illegal but I will let her go. The lower orders are beginning to think that they are not bound by any law. I don't much regret her, as she's stupid, fat and no great cook – but it is difficult to put anyone in her place at a moment's notice.'

The Diary of Colonel James Stevenson, 6 March 1924

Maid and Mistress

Not all employers were inconsiderate to their domestic staff and some engendered real loyalty. Mrs Ronald Greville had a devoted personal maid she called 'the Archduchess' because of her aristocratic air. In *The Sweet and Twenties* Beverley Nichols recalls walking into the Café Royal and seeing Mrs Ronnie, dressed in a black dress, dining with the Archduchess. 'There was nothing incongruous or embarrassing about it,' he commented. 'The two women were not only mistress and maid, they were friends.'

One trick of the ambitious hostess was to poach the best staff from her rivals. America heiress Grace Vanderbilt – or so an outraged Mrs Ronnie believed – had plans to 'entice away the Archduchess'.

'She may be rich, but she's not as rich as *that*!' she told Beverley Nichols. 'And in any case, it is not a question of money. I don't believe the Archduchess would leave me even if Gracie was to offer her a million dollars.'

Modern Technology

Luckily for those working 'below stairs' in the twenties, the gruelling daily grind of their work was slowly changing. The 1920s saw the invention and widespread adoption of a host of labour-saving devices that transformed homes – and lives – across the world.

With the introduction of domestic electricity, inventions such as the electric iron sprang forth, as innovators sought to exploit the vast opportunities provided by this new form of household power. During the early 1920s, the old flat iron all but disappeared; and by 1929, a survey of 100 households found that 98 of them owned electric irons.

Whether the creation of such labour-saving devices was partly inspired by the servant problem, allowing middle-class women to survive without staff, or merely hastened the end of a centuries-old way of life, is open to question. Nevertheless, the impact of domestic modernisations like the washing machine, central heating and even soap powder revolutionised people's lives. The strong arm of change was reaching everyone, and every aspect of life – even in the field of architecture.

New Homes

The combination of the cultural shift to day staff and the advent of labour-saving devices meant that middle-class homes were now being built without servants' quarters. Builders encouraged potential buyers with boasts of huge savings. The following claims appeared in a brochure for new homes in Beckenham, Kent, in 1920:

SERVANTS

It will be readily seen that with the labour-saving devices we are supplying with these houses, a domestic servant would be quite unnecessary, and apart from the advantage of being free from the troubles and inconveniences usually prevailing where maids are employed, it is interesting to note the financial aspect and see what is actually saved where their services are dispensed with.

Wages	(say)	£35
Keep	"	£65
Breakages	"	£4
		£104

or £2 a week apart from the question of extra light and heat consumed.

Stately Homes

Nevertheless, in the larger houses, residential staff remained a necessity. The dearth of willing souls was becoming a huge issue for the upper classes. From 1920, the government tackled this thorny problem by launching official 'home-craft' courses – with the condition the pupil would then become a servant – in an attempt to coax women back into service.

They even offered to pay for the first batch of uniforms, as many young girls were forced to work for up to two years to meet the considerable cost of the black dresses and starched white aprons required, which was understandably a significant career deterrent.

Bright Young Servants

In London, the frantic nightlife of the Mayfair set and their ilk provided a golden opportunity for a few who may otherwise have served tables in stately homes for a pittance. Nightclub owner Mrs Meyrick maintained that her waiters and dance hostesses often made more than she did from the generous tips of the sozzled socialites. At her famous 43 Club, she estimated that each member of staff made between £25 and £50 a week – considerably more than the £1 a week most maids would be getting.

Speak Easy

'Just six months [after I took on a new pageboy] I happened to be strolling along Bond Street when a smartly dressed youngster passed me. He took off his hat and smiled and a moment later I saw him getting into an expensive-looking motorcar, carefully hitching up his trousers as he sat down in order not to spoil their immaculate creases... It was my page. With the tips he had made in my club he had in the short space of half a year raised himself from the gutter to comfort and luxury.'

Mrs Meyrick remembers one down-and-out lad whom she took on as a pageboy because her head waiter said he was 'literally on the brink of starvation', *Secrets of the 43 Club*

Cooking Up a Storm

One former servant who escaped a life of relentless grind became a key part of the Bright Young People's social whirl. Rosa Lewis was a former kitchen maid from the East End who had worked her way up to the position of cook in a stately home, then became the equivalent of a celebrity chef. Finally, she opened the Cavendish Hotel in Jermyn Street, a favourite late-night drinking venue of the smart set.

Who's That Girl? Rosa Lewis

— ★ —

Famous For: As owner of the Cavendish Hotel, she earned the nickname Duchess of Jermyn Street and inspired the TV series *Duchess of Duke Street*.

— ★ —

Career Notes: Having gone into domestic service as a young girl, she worked her way up the servants' ranks and became the head of the kitchen for the wealthy Duke of Orleans. After learning French cuisine, she set up a successful mobile cooking service for rich households, and even cooked for King Edward VII. In 1902, she bought the Cavendish, which quickly became a fashionable haunt for the upper classes. Evelyn Waugh modelled hotel hostess Lottie Crump, in *Vile Bodies*, on Rosa – and was promptly barred from Rosa's establishment.

— ★ —

Sound Bite: Anthony Powell, who wrote a book entitled *A Bottle of Wine at the Cavendish*, recalled a seedy, slightly faded glamour about Rosa's parlour, and a 'tense, menacing atmosphere', not lessened by the fact that the hostess was prone to producing a bill to cover the drinks of all her guests and insisting the richest man in the room stump up for the lot!

MODERN
TIMES

> *I couldn't have electricity in the house,
> I wouldn't sleep a wink. All those vapours
> floating about.*

Lady Grantham, as played by
Dame Maggie Smith, in *Downton Abbey*

The post-war period sparked a new explosion of consumerism
as the middle-class housewife and the moneyed set were
bombarded with advertisements
for new gadgets, household
appliances and cleaning
products. Convenience foods
such as custard powder, stock
cubes and packet cereals
flooded the shops and the
advent of home electricity
added to the move towards
the servantless house. Times
they were a-changing.

In the Can

One of the innovations of the twenties which made the life of the housewife and servant a little easier was tinned food. Although the concept had been invented by French confectioner Nicolas Appert back in 1809 – in order to feed soldiers in the Napoleonic wars – the cost of producing the handmade cans was prohibitively high, and only the Army and Navy used the new preservation technique.

However, in the 1920s, the mass production lines pioneered by Henry Ford made canned food commercially viable for the first time and it became ubiquitous in every kitchen. The new process meant that a wide variety of fruit and vegetables, such as peas, corn and pears, could now be bought in tins, as well as whole meals, such as Heinz spaghetti in meatballs – or even dressed lobster.

Heinz baked beans with pork, which had first made it onto the shelves of Fortnum and Mason in 1886 as a high-priced delicacy, now became a staple on shopping lists in the UK.

Electric Shock

A building boom after the First World War meant more houses were wired for electricity but, at first, it was a scary prospect. Housewives wondered nervously how this magical form of power could come into their homes, lighting rooms, heating irons and ovens and making vacuum cleaners roar into life.

Magazines ran daily columns on cooking with electricity and Wilfred L Randell wrote a whole book of propaganda, called *The Romance of Electricity*. In 1924 Catherine Haslett even formed a pressure group called the Electrical Association for Women, which ran cookery classes using electric ovens.

By the end of the decade, over 1 million electric cookers were in use in British homes.

See the Light

Electricity marked the end of an era. In Deborah Mitford, the Duchess of Devonshire's book, *Chatsworth: The House*, footman Henry Bennett recalls the dimly lit twenties at the family's other homes, where electricity had not yet been installed: 'When we moved to Bolton Abbey (in Yorkshire) or Hardwick (Derbyshire), there was no electric light: oil lamps and candles were the order. A man was kept to see that the lamps contained oil, wicks trimmed and lamp glasses cleaned. It was the footman's duty to put lamps around the house. His Grace invariably liked candles, so quite a number of lighted candles adorned his study.'

Electricity was not regarded with such suspicion in the US. In 1917, only a quarter (24.3 per cent) of homes had been electrified, but by 1920 this figure had doubled (47.4 per cent), and by the end of the decade it had risen to four-fifths.

'Cheap Electricity for All'

In 1920 only 6 per cent of Britain's homes were connected with electricity, which was hardly surprising – it cost the equivalent of an average week's wage to keep five bulbs burning for a day. Conservative Prime Minister Stanley Baldwin came up with a solution in the 1926 Electricity Supply Act, which set up a National Grid to connect the 122 most efficient power stations in the country. The plan worked as more and more households found they could afford what was hailed as 'Cheap electricity for all'. By 1939, two-thirds of households were on the grid.

With the growing popularity of electricity came a boom on new appliances for the home, which would eventually replace the general maid in middle-class homes and help the staff in the larger homes – as long as employers were kind enough to invest.

A Timeline of Innovation

1920   handheld hairdryer invented in Germany, weighing over 2lbs

1920   sticky plasters invented by Earle Dickson, USA

1923   first 'portable' hearing aid developed using vacuum tubes, England

1924   frozen food invented by American Clarence Birdseye

1926   aerosol sprays, by Norwegian Erik Rotheim
1927   television, by John Logie Baird
1927   first quartz clock built by Warren Marrison and J W
        Horton at Bell Telephone Laboratories
1927   'talkies' hit the cinemas
1928   first machine-sliced bread on sale in Chillicothe,
        Missouri

Spick and Span

The put-upon maid was swiftly being replaced by the vacuum cleaner. Carpet sweepers had been on the market for a while but the twenties saw the vacuum become a fixture in the ordinary home. The disposable filter bag was introduced in 1920, and the invention of the upright vacuum cleaner followed six years later.

Cylinder vacuum cleaners were all the rage and a patronising advertisement from Electrolux, in 1926, implored housewives to invest in 'new cleanness' to rid themselves of the dangerous 'dusties'. It read:

> Are the 'dusties' settled in your house? Electrolux will clean them out. The 'dusties' are the germs that breed in dust. Get rid of the dust before it makes your home a centre of infection ... The old cleaning methods are worse than useless.

It also appealed to their pocket, with the claim: 'It works easily swiftly and thoroughly at a cost of less than 1d an hour.'

But the machines themselves weren't particularly cheap – in 1921 a Croydon vacuum cleaner cost £12 12s (£436 today) with added attachments for upholstery adding another £3 3s (£109) to the bill. In other words it cost just slightly less than the annual wage of a young housemaid. A Hoover – with its famous motto 'It beats, as it sweeps, as it cleans' – was a similar price.

Wash Day Blues

Another boon to the 'servantless home' was the electric washing machine, which began to become more popular towards the end of the decade. Built initially from wood and later with perforated metal, they had a revolving tub to do away with the need to scrub, and often had a mangle mounted on top to squeeze the water out after washing. A US company offering demonstrations of these modern-day marvels observed, in a 1920 advert:

> *A real servant in the home is a rarity in these days of complex labour conditions. The 1900 Cataract Electric Washer is a real servant that never goes on a strike, never demands more pay, and never tires with extra work.*

The Ice Age Cometh

The twenties also saw the introduction the first widely available electric refrigerator such as the Frigidaire Icebox, which promised to stay 'colder than ice' even in the height of

summer. The first models were actually timber framed but the late twenties saw all-steel casing coming in. The drawback was that the basic Frigidaire model cost around £64 – around £3,000 in today's money.

In 1927, American company General Electric produced the hugely popular Monitor Top – so called because it had a circular element on top of the main cabinet which meant it resembled the gun turret on the warship USS *Monitor*. Imagine having that in your kitchen!

By the end of the decade, 60 per cent of households in the US owned a refrigerator. It took the United Kingdom another forty years to achieve the same figure. Even so, 220,000 had been installed in British homes by 1931, along with 60,000 washing machines and 400,000 vacuum cleaners.

Motoring Along

Although cars had been manufactured since the late nineteenth century, they were seen as a rich man's toy before the First World War and much ridiculed by the majority. The wealthy aristocrat with more money than sense, who spent a fortune on motors that went no faster than a horse, was the model for Toad of Toad Hall in Kenneth Grahame's 1908 novel *The Wind in the Willows*:

> *'Then you don't promise,' said the Badger, 'never to touch a motor-car again?'*
>
> *'Certainly not!' replied Toad emphatically. 'On the contrary, I faithfully promise that the very first motor-car I see, poop-poop! Off I go in it!'*

Driving Sales

By the twenties, however, the mass production first introduced by Henry Ford in the United States had considerably reduced costs in Britain too. A Renault advert in 1926 offered the open-topped 13.9 horsepower English Torpedo for £375 (£17,000 today) and its Saloon model for £396 (£17,900). But a less powerful model was also available for £219, the equivalent of around £10,000 today.

Sales of motorcars boomed through the twenties and, by 1930, the number of private cars in Britain totalled 1,056,000, with motor vehicles, including tractors, buses and taxes, numbering 2,287,000. Two million people were employed in the motor industry.

Road Trips

While still out of reach of the working class, cars were now easily affordable for professionals and the upper classes. As reports of the treasure hunts showed, the Bright Young Things of the Mayfair set took 'motors' for granted, and delighted in the freedom they brought. Their weekends in the country now meant less tedious train travel and the possibility of 'popping down' for one night rather than doing a whole three-day stint arose.

Night Riders

Barbara Cartland recalled one paper chase in which she took part during the early hours of the morning:

> *There were fifty cars and we all assembled on the Horse Guards Parade and then went racing down the road, juggling and jostling for position. So it was very lucky it was 2 a.m., and that there was practically no traffic.*
>
> *Most of the cars were open so the girls' hair got blown about. As the men drove they often stood up to wave and shout at their friends. By the time we had crawled about on a pavement near Seven Dials, our dresses were dirty and some even managed to get them torn. It was a blessing there were no photographers!*

Motorbikes also became a popular and cheaper option for the younger man, with ownership rising 609,000 through the decade to 724,000. Fast-living young ladies delighted on hitching a ride on these mean machines — sitting on the metal grill at the back, which soon became known as the 'flapper bracket'.

Life in the Fast Lane

The modern age, with its fast cars, aeroplanes and gadgets, provided a fascination for the Bright Young Things, as well as a means of mobility. The proliferation of cars meant getting away for the weekend, as well as taking part in scavenger hunts, while the dawning of the commercial aviation age ensured the wealthiest traveller could now charter flights to fashionable locations such as the French Riviera and Monaco.

Motor racing was becoming a hugely popular sport with Grand Prix races, which originated in France, springing up in Italy (1921), Spain and Belgium (1924) and finally Britain (1926). Life in the twenties was all about faster, bigger, better, brighter – and modern technology more than kept up the breathless pace.

AIN'T WE GOT FUN

❝ If you can dream it, you can do it. ❞

Walt Disney

For the fun-loving set of the jazz age, it was the perfect era in which to be living life to the full. Just as modern inventions were revolutionising home life, the march of progress was also making itself felt in the world of show business, with radio and cinema leading the way with new innovations, and stagecraft becoming ever more entertaining.

Radio Makes Waves

Although Marconi had patented the first radio in 1896, transmission was banned in most countries between 1914 and 1918 and the 'wireless' didn't take off in the UK until well after the First World War. But throughout the twenties its growth worldwide was phenomenal. In the US, for example, between 1923 and 1930, 60 per cent of families bought radio sets.

The Birth of the BBC

On 14 November 1922, the first news bulletin from the British Broadcasting Corporation was broadcast from Marconi House in the Strand. It was read by the Director of Programmes, Arthur Burrows, who read each bulletin twice – once quickly and once slowly, so that listeners could decide which they preferred. The bulletin contained a speech by the Conservative leader Bonar Law and details of Old Bailey sessions, a train robbery, the sale of a Shakespeare folio, fog in London and 'the latest billiards scores'.

Apparently he found the whole experience exhausting. Quoted in *The Story of Broadcasting* by Richard Burrows, he later wrote, 'I am prepared to assert that there is no more exacting test of physical fitness and nervous condition than the reading of a news bulletin night after night to the British Isles.' Five years later the private company, led by John (later Lord) Reith, received a charter from the government 'to educate, to entertain and to inform' and became a non-commercial company.

As well as news, there were light-entertainment programmes, using talent from the music halls of the era, and dance music was also broadcast.

As the radio boom continued in the UK, the royal family saw that it could be used to reach subjects in all walks of life. King George V made his first broadcast at the opening of the Wembley Empire exhibition on 23 April 1924. Millions gathered round their radio sets to hear his voice for the first time and traffic on Oxford Street was stopped as crowds gathered to listen on loud speakers.

Richer Sounds

Although more and more homes were acquiring a radio set throughout the 1920s, they weren't cheap. On top of manufacturing costs, listeners would buy a 10 shilling (£22.20 today) 'receiving' licence and would then pay two further tariffs. The first was based upon the various components in the receiver and went to the BBC. The second was a levy of 12s 6d (£27.80) per valve, which went to the Marconi Co. as a royalty.

An advert from W G Pye radio manufacturers had the following prices for a basic 'two valve receiving set'. Today's equivalent is in brackets:

Price inc royalties (no valves)	£12 10s (£601)
Price inc headphones, batteries, valves etc and all royalties	£18 10s (£823)
Two valve-power amplifier of similar design	£19 10s (£867)

The Silent Silver Screen

After the drab, depressing days of the war, Britons craved laughter and glamour – and Hollywood had plenty to give. Stars like Gloria Swanson, Norma Shearer, Louise Brooks, Clara Bow and Mary Pickford had young audiences sighing with admiration and leading men Rudolph Valentino and Douglas Fairbanks quickened the pulse of many a girl with romance on her mind. Slapstick comedies had the filmgoers flocking to the picture houses in their thousands.

But never a word was spoken. The twenties was the golden age of the silent movie.

Speak Easy

'Adding sound to movies would be like putting lipstick on the Venus de Milo.'

Film actress Mary Pickford

Tinseltown

The first Hollywood studio, Nestor, had cranked up its cameras in 1911 and by the dawn of the jazz age decade, the Los Angeles suburb had established itself as the hub of the film industry, the 'dream factory'. Major studios run by the Warner Bros, Samuel Goldwyn, Louis B Mayer and William Fox had sprung up as well as Universal Studios and comedy specialists Keystone, producers of the 'Keystone Cops' series.

Roaring with Laughter

Silent slapstick was big business for the studios and Charlie Chaplin, Harold Lloyd and Buster Keaton were the kings of comedy. London-born Chaplin brought them flocking with movies such as *The Kid* (1921) and *The Gold Rush* (1923) while Buster – known as the Great Stone Face – set up his own production company in 1921 and starred in silent classics such as *The General* (1926) and *The Cameraman* (1928).

Harold Lloyd had played luckless down-and-outs in short films before the twenties but, having created the new persona of a fearless young man capable of anything – with the simple aid of a pair of black-rimmed glasses – he moved into feature films in 1921 with the successful *Sailor-Made Man* (1921) and

Grandma's Boy (1922). A year later came *Safety Last*, which included the classic scene of Harold clinging from the hands of a clock at the top of a skyscraper he had just climbed. By the mid-twenties Harold was earning around $1.5 million – the equivalent of $18.7 million today.

Joseph Frank Keaton VI was dubbed 'Buster' by family friend Harry Houdini after he fell down a flight of stairs at the age of six months and was unharmed. Being the master of escapology, Houdini knew a thing or two about the art of getting out of sticky situations without a scratch.

Vamps and Flappers

In the years leading up the twenties, Theda Bara had made the vamp look fashionable, with the skimpy clothing, the black-rimmed eyes and blood red lips of costume dramas such as *Cleopatra* and *Salome*. Gloria Swanson carried on the tradition in such movies as *Sadie Thompson* (1928) and *Queen Kelly* (1929) produced by her lover, Joseph Kennedy, the father of future president John F Kennedy. Towards the end of the decade, Greta Garbo had added her smouldering good looks to the movie billboards, playing the femme fatale in both silent and talking films.

Who's That Boy? Charlie Chaplin

— ★ —

Famous For: The character of the Tramp and box-office hits including *The Kid*, *The Gold Rush* and *The Great Dictator*. He also wrote the classic song 'Smile'.

— ★ —

Career Notes: Having grown up in poverty in London, Charles Chaplin moved to Hollywood at the age of twenty-four and was hired by Keystone. After borrowing Fatty Arbuckle's trousers and a derby hat, he invented the character of the Little Tramp, who debuted in the 1914 movie *Kid Auto Races at Venice*. In 1919, he formed United Artists with Mary Pickford, Douglas Fairbanks and D W Griffith. He enjoyed huge success throughout the twenties and even survived the advent of 'the talkies'. The first time the voice of the Tramp was heard was at the end of the 1936 movie, *Modern Times*. His movie career came to an abrupt halt in 1952 when, targeted by McCarthy's witch-hunt, he left the US and settled in Switzerland.

— ★ —

Sound Bite: Charlie once said: 'A day without laughter is a day wasted.'

Who's That Girl? Greta Garbo

— ★ —

Famous For: Swedish actress and queen of the silent era, she starred in hit movies *Flesh and the Devil* and *A Woman of Affairs*.

— ★ —

Career Notes: Signed up by Louis B Mayer in 1925, she moved to the US and made her first Hollywood movie, *The Torrent*, in 1925. In 1927, she made *Flesh and the Devil* and the chemistry with co-star John Gilbert, both on and off screen, made her the talk of Tinseltown and darling of the gossip columns. As 'the talkies' arrived, Greta took lessons to modify her Swedish accent and her husky, seductive tones made her a hit with audiences all over again. She retired from the screen in 1941 and lived a reclusive life until her death in 1990.

— ★ —

Sound Bite: She denied she ever uttered the quote most often attributed to her: 'I never said, "I want to be alone." I only said, "I want to be left alone." There is all the difference.'

First Film Flapper

Clara Bow, Louise Brooks and Joan Crawford all personified the flapper on screen but the first actress to claim the title lived the life both on and off the screen, and all too briefly. In 1920, Olive Thomas starred as a rebellious schoolgirl in *The Flapper*. The wild actress was revelling in the party lifestyle long before the Roaring Twenties, with husband Jack Pickford, brother of screen icon Mary Pickford. The pair were renowned for their drink and drugs binges and the twenty-six-year-old actress died in a hotel room shortly after *The Flapper* was released when she accidentally drank mercury bichloride solution, prescribed as an external ointment for Jack's syphilis.

Pick of the Bunch

Besides Charlie Chaplin, Mary Pickford was the biggest box office star of all. Dubbed 'Little Mary' and 'America's Sweetheart', she played everything from young innocent girls to prostitutes – and always for a handsome salary. By 1918, Mary was earning $10,000 a week – the equivalent of over $1 million today – but she declared that was not enough and moved to First National Studios for $675,000 ($6.8 million today). By 1922 she was Hollywood's first millionaire star.

After setting up United Artists with Charlie Chaplin, D W Griffith and her future husband Douglas Fairbanks, Mary starred in some of the biggest movies of the silent era, including *Polyanna* (1920), *Rosita* (1923) and *Little Lord Fauntleroy* (1921), in which she played both the little boy and his widowed mother.

> In 1929, Mary Pickford shocked her fans by appearing on screen with a fashionable bob, having cut off her trademark ringlets in the wake of her mother's death.

My Fair Lady

In 1920, Mary married Douglas Fairbanks, the dashing star of such swashbuckling adventures as *The Mask of Zorro*. Their honeymoon in London and Paris caused riots, as fans jostled to see Hollywood's most glamorous couple, and their return to the US brought huge crowds to railway stations across the country to catch a glimpse of their idols, who were now 'Hollywood royalty'.

An invitation to Pickfair, their Beverly Hills mansion, was the most sought-after ticket in town and dignitaries from the White House often asked if it was possible to visit.

The careers of the couple both suffered with the advent of talking movies and they split in the early thirties after Fairbanks' affair with English socialite Lady Sylvia Ashley.

> Dinner guests at Pickfair included George Bernard Shaw, Noël Coward, H G Wells, F Scott Fitzgerald, Sir Arthur Conan Doyle, Albert Einstein, Lord Mountbatten and aviator Amelia Earhart. Charlie Chaplin, Fairbanks' best friend, was a frequent guest.

Idol Chatter

Whenever he was in London, another leading Hollywood star, Rudolph Valentino, made a beeline for the 43 Club, where 'his svelte figure and fascinating face used immediately to attract the attention of everyone in the place'. In *Secrets of the 43 Club,* Mrs Meyrick recalled a meeting between the actor and a young peeress, which she overheard from behind a screen where she was working:

> *It was perfectly obvious that the young woman was wildly in love with Valentino, and it was equally evident that he did not reciprocate her passion. She behaved like a silly girl, trying to draw him out on the subject of love and telling tedious stories about the marriage proposals she claimed to have received ... It was painful to listen to her making such a fool of herself ...*
>
> *A few nights later I heard this same peeress give her impression of Valentino. 'He's quite a decent young kid,' she said. 'But he hasn't got any particular depth of character.'*

Speak Easy

'To generalise on women is dangerous. To specialise on them is infinitely worse.'

Rudolph Valentino

Who's That Boy? Rudolph Valentino

— ★ —

Famous For: Romantic lead whose swarthy good looks earned him an army of female fans.

— ★ —

Career Notes: Born in Puglia, Italy, he emigrated to the States in 1913, at the age of eighteen. After a few bit parts in Hollywood he landed leading roles in *The Four Horsemen of the Apocalypse* (1921), *The Sheik* (1921), *Blood and Sand* (1922), *The Eagle* (1925) and *Son of the Sheik* (1926). His sudden death from complications following an emergency appendix operation, in 1926, caused mass hysteria among his fans. He was just thirty-one.

— ★ —

Sound Bite: 'Women are not in love with me but with the picture of me they see on the screen. I am merely the canvas on which women paint their dreams.'

Talkies

The Jazz Singer premiered on 6 October 1927, and sounded the death knell for silent movies. Al Jolson starred as a would-be jazz artist forced to defy his family to achieve his dream and, for the first time, the actor moved his lips as spoken dialogue was heard. The first words he spoke were, 'Wait a minute, wait a minute, you ain't heard nothin' yet! Wait a minute, I tell ya! You ain't heard nothin'!'

Doris Warner, the daughter of Warner Bros studio founder Harry, was at the New York screening and remembered that at these prophetic words 'the audience became hysterical'. Critic Robert E Sherwood, who reviewed the film, later said the dialogue scene between Jolson and co-star Eugenie Besserer was 'fraught with tremendous significance ... I for one suddenly realised that the end of the silent drama is in sight.'

The first full-length talkie was a huge hit, taking $2.6 million at the box office ($32 million today). Sadly none of the Warner Brothers were there to see the film premiere – Sam Warner died the day before the screening and his three brothers, Harry, Albert and Jack, returned to California for his funeral.

The film's massive budget of $422,000 (£5.3 million in today's terms) was a huge gamble for Harry Warner, who pawned his wife's jewellery and down-sized the family home to raise the cash. The gamble paid off and the world of cinema was changed for ever.

Suffering in Silence

Now that Al Jolson had spoken, the public were eager to hear the dulcet tones of their screen idols. But not all fared well in the talkies revolution. Studios introduced voice tests and many actors and actresses saw their contracts renegotiated or terminated. Louise Brooks, for example, walked out when her studio attempted to reduce her salary.

Accents were often a stumbling block, putting paid to the careers of Valentino's beautiful lover, Polish actress Pola Negri, and Mexican Ramon Novorra. Others, like John Gilbert and Douglas Fairbanks, found the parts drying up because their voices didn't match the screen persona. Clara Bow, whose image defined the twenties jazz age, was out of work because her thick Brooklyn accent didn't suit the celluloid.

Greta Garbo, Joan Crawford, Lon Chaney and Gloria Swanson were among the stars who made the transition to talkies and continued to enjoy huge Hollywood success.

Speak Easy

'If I were an actor with a squeaky voice, I would worry.'

Cinema critic Welford Beaton on the release
of *The Jazz Singer*

Greta Speaks

Garbo's first talkie, *Anna Christie* (1929), earned her an Oscar nomination and had one critic, Richard Watts of the NY *Herald Tribune*, raving that she had '... the voice of a Viking's daughter, inherited from generations of seamen who spoke against the roar of the sea, and made themselves heard ... [her voice is] a deep, husky, throaty contralto with fabulous poetic glamour.' Another wrote, 'Some of the strange mystery of the woman (you never visualize Garbo as saying words, and it is a breathless sort of shock when she speaks) is gone, but the new Garbo is a greater actress than the old.'

Making the Mickey

The 1928 animation *Steamboat Willie* saw the birth of a movie legend – Mickey Mouse. Inspired by a pet mouse on Walt Disney's farm, he was called Mortimer until Walt's wife, Lillian, persuaded him to change it. The cute little character and his beloved Minnie, both voiced by their creator, were an instant success and went on to star in many more cartoons, as the Disney empire grew from a tiny animation studio into a multi-million-dollar Hollywood giant. In years to come, Walt Disney would comment, 'I only hope that we never lose sight of one thing – that it was all started by a mouse.'

Speak Easy

'We felt that the public, and especially the children, like animals that are cute and little. I think we are rather indebted to Charlie Chaplin for the idea. We wanted something appealing, and we thought of a tiny bit of a mouse that would have something of the wistfulness of Chaplin – a little fellow trying to do the best he could.'

Walt Disney, quoted in *Disney and His Worlds* by Alan Bryman

A Talent to Amuse

After a wartime slump, the theatres of the West End sprang back to life in the twenties and, like the rest of London, the stage became a celebration of youth, with bright new talents producing witty plays and cheerful revues to capture the mood.

Ivor Novello and P G Wodehouse produced musical comedies like *The Golden Moth* but the brightest star of the 1920s theatre scene was Noël Coward. Outrageous, flamboyant and wonderfully witty, the playwright and sometime actor epitomised the high life of the Bright Young People and, while he kept his homosexuality behind closed doors, he revelled in his image as an immoral bohemian. He once told the *Evening Standard*, 'I am never out of opium dens. My mind is a mass of corruption.'

Who's That Boy? Noël Coward

— ★ —

Famous For: Becoming the voice of high society with plays like *The Vortex*, *Easy Virtue* and *Hay Fever*, as well as witty songs including 'Mad Dogs and Englishmen' and 'I Went to a Marvellous Party'.

— ★ —

Career Notes: After nine months serving with the Artists' Rifles during the Great War, Noël suffered a nervous breakdown and was discharged. He recovered while enjoying the country houses of friends and family, which would become the basis of his work, before starring in his own play, *I'll Leave It to You* at the age of twenty, in 1920. A spell in New York inspired him further and he went on to gain huge success in 1924 with *The Vortex*, followed by *Hay Fever*, *Fallen Angels* and *On With the Dance*, which starred David Tennant's wife Hermione, in 1925. *Easy Virtue* followed a year later and his career bloomed well into the thirties and forties, with memorable plays such as *Private Lives* and *Blithe Spirit*.

— ★ —

Sound Bite: Barbara Cartland said: 'Noël became the high priest of "the wicked twenties".'

The Bright Young Things adored the playful playwright and were often among his early audiences and most ardent fans. When his second play, *The Young Idea*, opened in the West End, reviewers recalled the high spirits of Noël's followers. 'Mr Noël Coward calls his brilliant little farce a "comedy of youth", and so it is. And youth pervaded the Savoy last night, applauding everything so boisterously that you felt, not without exhilaration, that you were in the midst of a "rag",' wrote one critic – while another complained, 'I was unfortunately wedged in the centre of a group of his more exuberant friends who greeted each of his sallies with "That's a Noëlism!"'

Speak Easy

'I was unwise enough to be photographed in bed wearing a Chinese dressing gown and an expression of advanced degeneracy. This last was accidental and was caused by blinking at the flashlight, but it emblazoned my unquestionable decadence firmly in the minds of all who saw it.'

Noël Coward, quoted in *We Danced All Night*
by Barbara Cartland

Come to the Cabaret

Cabaret had been born in 1881 at *La Chat Noir* (The Black Cat) in Montmartre. By the 1920s, the format had not only spread all over Europe, with cabaret clubs in London, Berlin and Amsterdam, but had produced many more infamous venues in Paris itself too. With hot jazz tunes, new-fangled choreography

and potent cocktails fuelling the fun, nights out had never been so entertaining.

The Moulin Rouge, with its iconic windmill on the roof, was destroyed by fire in 1915 but reopened in 1921 with a huge new show. Mistinguett, a beautiful French singer and actress – and the highest paid female entertainer of the time – headlined the sell-out revues, which often featured her younger lover, Maurice Chevalier.

In 1918, the Folies Bergère had been taken over by Paul Derval, who introduced more extravagant costumes and special effects, as well as the 'small nude women' who would become the venue's trademark as its success grew throughout the twenties. The shows often reflected the Parisian fascination with the black immigrants who now lived in the city. It was here, in 1926, that Josephine Baker became an overnight sensation with her *Danse Sauvage*, wearing a skirt made of a string of artificial bananas and little else.

Fabulous Folly

One of the most daring shows on Broadway was the *Ziegfeld Follies* at the New Amsterdam Theatre. Based on the famous Folies Bergère in Paris, the show was started in 1907 by impresario Florenz Ziegfeld and featured vaudeville acts, comedians, singers, and most importantly, scantily clad chorus girls. In the early twenties, the *Follies* were more popular than ever and the famous names to appear in the show included W C Fields and Fanny Brice. Showgirls, including future stars Barbara Stanwyck and Paulette Goddard, as well as flapper extraordinaire Louise Brooks, were hand-picked for their beauty and grace by notorious womaniser Ziegfeld, who enjoyed affairs with many of his protégées. They paraded on stage in a variety of costumes by top designers of the day and drew huge crowds, often leaving the show to marry wealthy admirers.

The annual Ziegfeld Ball, where many of the dancing girls met future husbands, continued as a social event of the season for years after the last production of the *Follies* in 1931.

Who's That Girl? Josephine Baker

— ★ —

Famous For: Erotic dance style and appearing on stage half naked.

— ★ —

Career Notes: Born in Missouri, USA, Josephine was introduced to vaudeville after she was spotted dancing for money on street corners at the age of fifteen. After a spell in Harlem, she moved to Paris to star at the Folies Bergère, causing a stir with her sensual dancing, comedic talent, uninhibited routines and barely-there costumes. She was the first African-American woman to become an international entertainer and was showered with gifts from admirers, including motorcars, precious gems, and more than 1,500 marriage proposals. She went on to become a leading supporter of the Civil Rights Movement in the US, and an active member of the French Resistance during the Second World War. She also raised twelve adopted children from various ethnic backgrounds.

— ★ —

Sound Bite: Ernest Hemingway called Josephine 'the most sensational woman anyone ever saw'.

Among the hopefuls who were turned down by Florenz Ziegfeld before going on to make it big elsewhere were Norma Shearer, Joan Crawford, Gypsy Rose Lee, Lucille Ball and Hedda Hopper.

The London Scene

Many of the 1920s London nightclubs provided more than a tipple and a chance to dance too. Musical entertainment was often laid on in the form of a cabaret, with dancing girls, musicians and singers. The trade in the UK clubs was given a boost by a 1923 law which banned bars at the old-fashioned music halls, meaning that those who could afford it, and wanted a drink with their evening's entertainment, deserted the traditional venues. Nightclub owners paid a premium for entertainers with a following who could attract the crowds.

Mrs Meyrick recalled in her memoirs, 'No cabaret turn is worth its place unless the performer has a large personal following, and artistes with a ready-made clientele do not appear in return for a pittance. When the Revellers sang at the Silver Slipper they asked for – and got – not merely a guaranteed salary but a substantial percentage of the profits as well. Once in a single year I spent £3,000 [£133,000 today] on pianos and no less than £10,000 [£445,000] on the musical entertainment of my guests. These figures appear almost fabulous, but they are accurate.'

The Kit Cat Club

The huge purpose-built Kit Cat Club opened in 1925 in Haymarket and was billed as 'luxurious, but wonderfully comfy ... a vastly patronised and fashionable resort'. Its membership soon exceeded 6,000, and included princes, cabinet ministers, dukes and peers.

As well as restaurants, bars and a huge dance floor, the club boasted the best cabaret in town, sharing acts with the nearby Piccadilly Hotel, which was owned by the same syndicate of investors. The headlining act for the grand opening were the famous American entertainers the Dolly Sisters, who were shortly to appear at the famous Moulin Rouge in Paris. It also featured the dancing duo of the deMarcos, Ted Lewis and his band, comedians Val and Ernie Stanton and celebrated dancers Sielle and Mills. Max Wall, singer Marion Harris and dancers Maurice and Eleanor Ambrose were among the famous faces of the era who entertained in the Kit Cat Club. But in December 1926, a year after it opened, the club was raided and the proprietors fined £500 (£22,600 today) each, plus £156 (£7,000) costs, for serving drinks out of licensing hours.

The venue reopened as a restaurant under new management in May 1927, but still boasted a glittering cabaret, including the internationally renowned dancer and comedian Johnny Hudgins – known as the Wah Wah Man because of his comedy mime act, which was always accompanied by sound effects from a jazz trumpet – and American singer and comedienne Sophie Tucker.

Board Games

Meanwhile, for those who stayed at home, and perhaps sought tamer pleasures, Monopoly, invented by Lizzie J Magie-Phillips as 'The Landlord's Game' in 1904, became a commercial success in 1923. However, the popular London version, featuring many of the favourite haunts of the Bright Young People, didn't appear until the 1930s. In the Mayfair drawing rooms, cards were still king – but one Asian import was becoming the very latest thing.

In *Grace and Favour*, Loelia Ponsonby wrote, 'The game of Mah-Jongh suddenly became all the rage and was played with the seriousness that was given to Canasta in 1950 and for a time it almost rivalled bridge in popularity ... One lady boasted that the Aga Khan had given her a white jade set costing several thousand pounds, but ours was only ivory backed with wood. Still it was very pretty.'

LET'S DO IT (LET'S FALL IN LOVE)

> *Another bride, another June, another sunny honeymoon.*
> *Another season, another reason, for Makin' Whoopee.*
>
> Gus Kahn, 'Makin' Whoopee'

Wild Wedding

One of the most notorious pranks pulled by the Bright Young People was the mock wedding party held at the Trocadero in 1929. Apparently the brainchild of the incorrigible Elizabeth Ponsonby, who played the part of the not-so-blushing bride, the wedding breakfast featured John Rayner as the groom and Robert Byron as the best man, resplendent in bowler hat and waxed moustache. Oliver Messel was an usher and Babe Plunkett-Greene a bridesmaid. One newspaper reported:

> *It was shortly after one o'clock that the patrons were interested to see the 'bride' arrive, holding a bouquet of*

165

perfect pink roses, escorted by a good-looking, but somewhat shy young 'bridegroom', immaculate from his waved hair to his striped shirt.

The spirited youngsters then roped in an unsuspecting clergyman, who happened to be enjoying lunch at the Piccadilly restaurant, and asked him to join them. He gave a blessing to the 'newly-weds' who were then showered with confetti and rose petals as they left. The 'bride and bridegroom' left 'for their honeymoon' in an ancient taxi-cab, to which some thoughtful friend had tied an even more ancient shoe.

This latest escapade gave the gossip writers a field day and sent shock waves through the London society because of its cheapening of the serious institution of marriage. Robert Byron's mother wrote to her son in horror, 'You are doing yourself harm with that sort of publicity – disgusting ... you have got some friends of the wrong sort, dear boy, and I wish you'd drop them.' Elizabeth's father, politician Arthur Ponsonby, wrote, 'E. again advertised in the paper at some absurd sort of party. It never stops.'

In an effort to promote his new invention, the pogo stick designer George Hansburg taught the Ziegfeld Girls to use it. In 1920, as a result, the *Ziegfeld Follies* featured a wedding performed on pogo sticks. There's a marriage with its ups and downs.

The Real Thing

Despite a seemingly frivolous attitude to marriage, the Bright Young People did expect to walk down the aisle for real at some point. In fact, Elizabeth herself wed a young shop owner named Denis Pelly six months after the mock wedding. In a world where the majority of careers were still closed to women, a good marriage was the most they could look forward to and magazines of the day were desperate to convince the young, independent woman that marriage was 'the best job of all'.

Working Towards the Wedding

As more single women went out to work, the journals of the day began reluctantly to accept the situation, but saw paid employment as a pathway to marriage. *Woman's Own*, for example, suggested that becoming a nurse, a library assistant or secretary could provide 'a short cut to a prosperous marriage'. The best occupation, in their opinion, was telephonist, because 'many a man falls in love with a voice'.

Courting the Debs

Despite the high jinks the Bright Young Men got up to at parties, those who wanted to win the heart of a lady were still expected to behave like gentlemen. Barbara Cartland recalled her first season after coming out: 'The young men I knew in 1919 and 1920 treated me as if I were made from Dresden china. They never swore in front of me. I was never told a risky story, they made no improper advances. To the men who asked me to dance I was a "lady" and entitled to respect.'

The future novelist said that a respectable woman was 'a thing apart, still to be wooed, before she was won. And how delightfully one was wooed. Men who loved me would stand outside my house late at night on the evenings I did not go out with them, in silent salute. Men who dropped me home in the early hours of the morning would leave a note a few hours later for me to find on my breakfast tray. They would write me poems and there would be flowers.'

For Better or Worse

By the end of the First World War, Britain had lost over 886,000 men, and those who remained unharmed were quickly snapped up. Not surprisingly, 1920 proved a bumper year for weddings, with over 100,000 more than ten years before, as the statistics below show:

Year	Number of weddings
1910	267,721
1920	379,982
1930	315,109

Coco Chanel's fashion influence extended to the wedding dress. She introduced a short, knee-length dress with a long train in 1920, which also cemented white, a popular choice already, as the universal colour of the wedding dress.

Royal Wedding

The marriage of Prince Albert, Duke of York to Lady Elizabeth Bowes-Lyon – later to become King George VI and Queen Elizabeth – was *the* society wedding of the 1920s. The bride, who had refused her Prince twice before finally agreeing in 1923, was technically a commoner so the blessing of the Royal Family and the political establishment signalled a more liberal outlook towards the old conventions.

The couple married on 26 April 1923 in Westminster Abbey, breaking with tradition by choosing a London church rather than a Royal chapel in the well-founded belief that the post-war society would have its spirits lifted by a public spectacle. The bride made a touching gesture in remembrance to the war dead, surprising guests by laying her bouquet at the Tomb of the Unknown Soldier. The wedding was also the first to be filmed, although the BBC were not allowed to broadcast it, as they'd hoped.

After the ceremony, the Duke and Duchess honeymooned at Mrs Ronald Greville's Surrey home, Polesden Lacey, before moving on to Scotland, where they both caught a rather unromantic bout of whooping cough.

Flapper Bride

Although it was floor length, Lady Elizabeth's wedding gown was a true flapper style statement, with flat front, dropped waist and lace detail. Designed by Queen Mary's dressmaker, Madame Handley Seymour, it was embroidered with pearls and silver thread, and the train was Flanders lace, a gift from Queen Mary.

Elizabeth's Scottish heritage was represented in a strip of lace, which had been worn by a Strathmore ancestor at a ball thrown for Bonnie Prince Charlie, which was sewn into the dress, and the silver leaf girdle, fastened with a silver thistle, which had a trail of spring green tulle.

Matched engagement and wedding bands were the height of fashion in the twenties, and square or lace mounts replaced the diamond solitaires of previous years. Plain gold bands were ditched in favour of carved designs, which were considered more youthful – a must if the Bright Young Things were to wed at all.

Bright Young Couple

Diana Mitford and Bryan Guinness were the most celebrated married couple of the Mayfair set. The hugely wealthy Irish aristocrat, who would become Baron Moyne, met the legendary beauty at a fancy dress ball at her home when she was just sixteen and, according to his friend Robert Byron, was soon 'grotesquely in love'. The couple were secretly engaged in July 1928 and finally wed in January 1929, when Diana was just eighteen and Bryan twenty-three. The young couple enjoyed a huge annual income of £20,000 (around £950,000 today), an estate in Hampshire, and houses in London and Dublin.

As the wealthiest and most adored of their circle, the couple hosted legendary parties at their London home and their set provided much of the fodder for *Vile Bodies*, which Evelyn Waugh – who once declared that Diana's beauty 'ran through the room like a peal of bells' – dedicated to them both.

Hostages to Fortune

Not everyone approved of the Mitford-Guinness union. Diana's parents believed the vast fortune would be too much for the newly-weds to handle and Robert Byron noted that, 'Diana Mitford is particularly charming, very pretty and amusing,' but added that 'the truth of it all is that Bryan is still monstrously young' and believed that his friend had fallen for 'a girl who will soon be much older than he can be'.

Although the couple had two sons, the marriage was short-lived. In 1932, Diana began a public affair with fascist leader Oswald Mosley, whom she went on to marry.

Acting Up

Mixing in the circles they did, favouring actresses and artists, the smart set were always in danger of falling for the 'wrong sort'. Actresses and showgirls were a particular bête noir of upper-class parents and Lord Robert Innes-Ker, the son of the Dowager Duchess of Roxburghe, was one who fell for such charms, marrying English actress José Collins, star of hit musical *Maid of the Mountains*, in 1920.

The following American newspaper report illustrates the general disapproval of such a union:

> *Bobby Innes-Ker is always a gay and reckless character and his intimacy with actresses and music-hall favourites has existed for years, but it was hoped he wouldn't marry into the footlights out of consideration for his distinguished relations. Queen Mary probably would not care to receive Miss José Collins, even when disguised as Lady Robert Innes-Ker, when, on the other hand, the future king would certainly be very pleased to meet her.*

A survey by American biologist Alfred Kinsey found that the number of women having sex before marriage doubled in the twenties. He found that 50 per cent of women born between 1900 and 1909 were not virgins on their wedding day, compared to around 25 per cent before the First World War. The majority of those women, however, had only had sex with their fiancé.

He-Evelyn and She-Evelyn

In June 1928, Evelyn Waugh wed Evelyn Gardner at St Paul's Church in Portman Square, despite vocal opposition from the bride's mother, Lady Brughclere. Among those present were Harold Acton, Robert Byron, Waugh's brother Alec and Miss Gardner's friend Pansy Pakenham, but the ill-fated marriage lasted no more than a year.

She-Evelyn was taken ill on a Mediterranean cruise the following summer and shortly afterwards returned to London, while He-Evelyn repaired to the country to write *Vile Bodies*. A month later, she informed her husband she had fallen in love with Jonathan Heygate, an aristocratic BBC announcer, and she promptly moved her belongings into her lover's flat. Heygate was consequently forced out of the BBC for his part in the divorce.

Speak Easy

'I did not know it was possible to be so miserable and live.'

A devastated Waugh on his wife leaving him, to Harold Acton

Grounds for Divorce

The demands of women's rights movements for equality in divorce led to the 1923 Matrimonial Causes Act, which made adultery by either husband or wife the sole ground for divorce. This meant that a wife no longer had to prove additional faults against the husband.

The change in the law led to a rise in cases of around 43 per cent from 2,800 in the early 1920s to 4,000 a year in the latter years. Society still frowned on divorce, however, and while the upper classes seemed to tolerate endless infidelities, the majority of the older generation nevertheless believed marriage was for life.

In the US, the latter part of the decade saw divorce rates rise to eight per thousand marriages per year, from four at the turn of the century.

Marital Mystery

When writer Agatha Christie was told by Colonel Archie Christie, her husband of twelve years, that he was having an affair and no longer loved her, she took the perfect revenge. In December 1926, she left her home, abandoned her car at Guildford, and 'disappeared'. In fact she was staying at a hotel in Harrogate under the false name of Miss Neale – the name of her husband's lover.

The eleven days in which the well-known novelist was missing put the spotlight firmly on her errant husband and even led to speculation he had murdered her. The newspapers had a field day and Archie suffered huge social embarrassment. They eventually divorced in 1928.

Virgin Birth

When Christabel Russell found out she was pregnant it led to the most notorious divorce case of the decade. Her husband, the Honourable John Hugo Russell, claimed that, at his wife's request, they had never had full sex and therefore the baby could not be his. In 1922, he sued her for divorce on the grounds of infidelity.

In turn, she argued that they had indulged in heavy petting which could have led to the pregnancy, and the doctors who attended her during pregnancy told the court her hymen was intact. Even so, three men were named in court as Christabel's lovers and she herself wrote to a friend, 'I have been so frightfully indiscreet all my life that he has enough evidence to divorce me about once a week.'

The first court ruled the evidence inconclusive, the second ruled in her husband's favour but a fresh appeal, tried in the House of Lords, overturned the decision and declared the child legitimate.

Keep Young and Beautiful

Despite the change in the law, magazines such as *Good Housekeeping*, *Woman's Own* and *Woman* magazine still took the view that a straying husband was the fault of the wife, who was expected to make the most of her appearance after marriage.

One *Woman's Own* article warned women to 'stop to think how often these lapses on the part of a devoted husband are due to the fact that their wives refuse to dress up for them ...

it was your face, the physical charm of you which made you attractive and winsome to the man.'

Sex and Scandal

But despite the best efforts of the women's magazines, the fact was that the increasingly public infidelities and widespread divorces were a sign of the times. As it would turn out, no amount of face cream could hold back the tide of immoral behaviour once the twenties really started to roar ...

MAKIN' WHOOPEE

> *I feel quite sure, an affaire d'amour*
> *Would be attractive*
> *While we're still active, let's misbehave!*
>
> Cole Porter, 'Let's Misbehave'

Single flappers may have been shocking society with their disreputable behaviour, but in truth the majority were quite chaste compared to some of their married counterparts. The Bright Young People's public displays of uproarious rebellion filled the gossip columns – but the real scandals of the 1920s were taking place behind closed doors ...

The Happy Valley Set

Colonial Kenya, in the 1920s, was a wild playground for rich and powerful ex-pats who were dubbed the Happy Valley Set. Their drinking, drug use and wife-swapping were notorious and nights at the Muthaiga Country Club in Nairobi were followed by shocking parties in their palatial homes. Their outrageous behaviour would lead to many scandals throughout the twenties and beyond ...

The Bolter

Idina Sackville travelled to Kenya with second husband Captain Charles Gordon after her marriage in 1919 and quickly took to the hedonistic lifestyle, taking a stream of lovers from the club.

When her marriage foundered, she returned to London, where she caused further scandal by embarking a high-profile affair with Josslyn Hay, Earl of Errol, whom she married in 1923. Together they travelled back to Kenya where it transpired that Errol, eight years her junior, was as promiscuous as his new wife.

The pair hosted all-night parties at their sprawling bungalow above the Rift valley, and Idina was said to welcome her guests in a bathtub made of green onyx, before dressing in front of them.

After numerous affairs they split in 1930. Idina, thought to be the model for the character of 'The Bolter' in three of Nancy Mitford's novels, would go on to marry twice more. Errol was shot after spending the night with his lover Lady Diana Broughton, in 1941. Her husband Jock Broughton was later acquitted of his murder.

Crimes of Passion

Count Frederic de Janze and his wife Alice travelled to the valley in 1925, at the invitation of the Errols, whom they met in Paris. Living next door to the Errols for several months,

Alice had a fling with Lord Errol while her husband bedded Idina.

Alice then left her husband for another lover, British baronet Raymond de Trafford. In 1927, the Countess shot her lover at a railway station in Paris and then shot herself. Both survived and Alice was fined $4. She later married Raymond.

She shot herself in Kenya in 1941, after the death of Lord Errol.

The Girl with the Silver Syringe

Alice Gwynne – nicknamed Kiki – was an American socialite who moved to Kenya in 1926 with her second husband and became notorious for her excessive use of cocaine and heroin. Dubbed 'the girl with the silver syringe' for her habit of shooting up in public, she also had numerous affairs, including a dalliance with Prince George, Duke of Kent, which caused much anguish to the royal family. She committed suicide in New York in 1946.

A Rather Racy Royal

The Prince of Wales's younger brother, George – not to be confused with the future George VI, whose real name was Albert – was another royal party animal. The Duke of Kent's numerous affairs – reportedly with both men and women – were the talk of the town. Among his conquests were black cabaret singer Florence Mills, banking heiress Poppy Baring and Margaret Wigham, later the Duchess of Argyll.

Rumours of a long-term affair with Noël Coward were denied by his partner Graham Payne, but other dalliances were thought to include the duke's distant cousin Louis Ferdinand, Prince of Prussia, and Anthony Blunt. According to *War of the Windsors: A Century of Unconstitutional Monarchy* by Picknett, Prince, Prior and Brydon, he also had a *ménage a trois* with Jorge Ferrara, the bisexual son of an Argentinian ambassador, while Alice Gwynne was believed to have borne him a secret lovechild.

Speak Easy

'No one dreamed for one instant of doing anything so banal as living with her own husband.'

> Noël Coward in a letter to Beverley Nichols about the Ritz Bar in Paris, as published in Nichols's *The Sweet and Twenties*

Gay Paris

The scandals of the Roaring Twenties spread across the globe – especially to Paris, where the heady glamour of the French capital caused many to lose their heads. In 1920 Nancy Cunard, the daughter of society hostess Emerald, scandalised society by running off to Paris and moving in with black jazz musician Henry Crowder.

Yet the flighty Nancy was by no means the only society flapper drawn to the bright lights and lifestyle of the French capital. Paris in the 1920s was a haven for hard-drinking Americans fleeing the Prohibition, as well as English aristocrats merely out to have a good time on the cheap, and it became *the* place to be.

Writers and artists such as F Scott Fitzgerald, Ernest Hemingway, Gertrude Stein and Picasso flocked to experience the Beau Monde, as the fashionable society of Paris was known, and the sense of personal freedom in the years following the First World War encouraged all manner of excess. Gambling dens were packed to the rafters, drink and drugs were readily available and the clubs of Montmartre offered saucy shows and scantily clad dancing girls — including the infamous Josephine Baker — the likes of which were never seen in the legal London clubs.

White Nights

As wild and hedonistic as the original Bright Young People were, their vices rarely ran to drugs. Cocaine was no doubt available at Mayfair parties — while some of the seedier nightclubs were awash with the stuff — but the smart set maintained a certain innocence in the 1920s.

Brian Howard, one of the more outrageous members, appeared rather shocked and pious on encountering a cocaine addict in Berlin, in 1927. In *Brian Howard: Portrait of a Failure*, Marie-Jacqueline Lancaster reports that the man returned to his oblivious wife and children, prompting Brian to observe, 'To think that tucked away in one of those capacious pockets lay a little folded slip of paper, or a little bottle, containing all the sugars of hell.'

Nightclub owner Mrs Meyrick, however, lost many a dancing girl to drug addiction and put the blame squarely on the infamous 'Brilliant' Chang.

Brilliant But Deadly

Chinese businessman Billy 'Brilliant' Chang was a London restaurant owner and a dangerous drug dealer, who appeared to have a magnetic power over women of the day. Mrs Meyrick recalled, 'Chang was one of the most unscrupulous characters of post-war London. His snake-like eyes and powerful personality used to fascinate nearly all the women he met – and all too often led to their downfall. He was undoubtedly the mastermind behind the drug traffic in England.'

The cunning Chinaman became a famous London figure, and when he opened a restaurant opposite the 43 Club, she found it increasingly difficult to 'keep a check on his evil influence'.

In 1922, Chang was implicated in the death of dance teacher Freda Kempton, from a cocaine overdose. Although the inquest could not prove a link, she had spent the evening at his establishment before her death.

His final downfall came two years later when police raided his Limehouse flat and found cocaine, as well as a stack of handwritten letters addressed to 'Dear unknown', inviting unsuspecting young ladies to meet him at his restaurant.

C'est Magnifique

On the whole, however, the rich and famous saved their drug-dabbling for trips to Europe, and in particular Paris. American songwriter Cole Porter maintained a lavish apartment in Paris, with walls covered in zebra hide, where he and his wife, Linda Lee Thomas, threw their decadent parties.

Despite being an outwardly devoted husband, Porter was gay and according to one biographer, J X Bell, his parties were notorious for 'gay and bisexual activity, Italian nobility, cross-dressing, international musicians, and a large surplus of recreational drugs'.

Tea Time

In the US, drugs were freely available in the speakeasies and drug addiction was rife among many jazz musicians, with marijuana, cocaine and morphine the most common narcotics.

In Lucy Moore's *Anything Goes*, saxophonist Milton 'Mezz' Mezzrow said, 'Tea [marijuana] puts a musician in a real masterly sphere, and that's why so many jazzmen used it. You hear everything at once and you hear it right. When you get that feeling of power and sureness, you're in a solid groove.'

Chicago mafia boss Al Capone ran lucrative drug rackets but was also addicted to cocaine. When he was finally jailed in 1931, he was found to have a perforated nasal septum, a result of overuse.

Mad About the Boy

While drugs were not widespread among the Bright Young Things, homosexuality – at that time still illegal and considered the worst kind of debauchery by the popular press – was rife.

Many, like Brian Howard, Stephen Tennant, Beverley Nichols and Eddie Gathorne-Hardy, were flamboyant peacocks who made no secret of their preferences among their closest friends. Nichols, for example, openly boasted to Cecil Beaton of his flings with writers Somerset Maugham, Oliver Messel and Noël

Coward. Others, like Cole Porter, were married to provide an outward air of respectability while continuing homosexual activity – with or without marital consent.

At universities and private schools, such as Eton, the sexually confused often went through a 'gay phase', seeing experimenting as a rite of passage. Evelyn Waugh, for example, had various affairs with men at Oxford before falling for a succession of high-society women. As John Betjeman once remarked, as quoted in Paula Byrne's biography of Waugh, *Mad World*: 'Everyone in Oxford was homosexual at that time.'

Speak Easy

'Nearly every English boy I knew had a terrific exposure to homosexuality. Some stuck with it, some didn't, but nobody paid much attention either way.'

Jessica Mitford in a letter to her friend Merle Miller in 1971, published in *Decca*, edited by Peter Sussman

Jazz Gigolo

Throughout the twenties and into the thirties, Leslie 'Hutch' Hutchinson was the talk of society drawing rooms throughout London and Paris. The black pianist's affairs with rich men and women caused numerous scandals and Cole Porter, reputed to be one of his many lovers, is thought to have based the 1929 song 'I'm a Gigolo' on Hutch.

Who's That Boy? Leslie 'Hutch' Hutchinson

— ★ —

Famous For: Scandalous affairs with such high-society figures as Ivor Novello and Lady Mountbatten.

— ★ —

Career Notes: The musician from Grenada travelled to Harlem when he was sixteen and played piano for Fats Waller and Duke Ellington, before moving to Europe in 1924, where he became a sought-after society entertainer. At a time of blatant racial discrimination, the West Indian headlined at the Café de Paris and Quaglino's, hobnobbed with the Prince of Wales, bought a house in Hampstead and drove a Rolls-Royce. Lady Edwina Mountbatten had a long dalliance with Hutch and reportedly lavished him with expensive gifts, such as a gold-and-diamond watch.

— ★ —

Sound Bite: A BBC producer told Hutch's biographer, Charlotte Breese: 'I was at a grand party. Edwina interrupted Hutch playing the piano. She kissed his neck and led him by the hand behind the closed doors of the dining-room. There was a shriek, and a few minutes later she returned, straightening her clothes. Hutch seemed elated, and before he returned to the piano, told me that, with one thrust, he had flashed [propelled] her the length of the dining-room table.'

Hutch caused outrage behind closed doors by getting debutante Elizabeth Corbett pregnant. Forced to marry a Guards officer when she was three months into pregnancy, she shocked her husband just before the birth by telling him the baby could be black. The child was given up for adoption.

School for Scandal

American actress Tallulah Bankhead's reputation for wild behaviour made her a darling of the Mayfair set but also brought her to the attention of MI5 – who suspected her of seducing schoolboys.

A dossier on the actress revealed that the Home Office asked the intelligence services to investigate rumours of 'indecent and unnatural' acts with several under-age boys at Eton College. She was also accused of being a lesbian, being promiscuous with men and of moving in a social circle that was a bed of vice.

The American star was saved from a public scandal by Eton's headmaster Dr C A Alington, who refused to co-operate with agents sent to interview him.

Concluding there was little evidence against her, the investigator, known as FHM, wrote: 'The headmaster is obviously not prepared to assist HO by revealing what he knows of her exploits with some of the boys, i.e. he wants to do everything possible to keep Eton out of the scandal.'

Who's That Girl? Tallulah Bankhead

— ★ —

Famous For: Starring roles in the West End and Hollywood. Also for sexual exploits, including numerous affairs, wild parties and cutting wit.

— ★ —

Career Notes: The daughter of an Alabama politician, she made her stage debut in New York, in 1918, at the age of sixteen. Five years later she moved to London where she spent eight years on the West End stage in such hit shows as *The Dancers* and the Pulitzer Prize winner *They Knew What They Wanted*. Forthright and liberated, she became a much coveted guest at the London parties. In 1931 she moved to Hollywood, where she made several movies.

— ★ —

Sound Bite: She once said she was 'as pure as the driven slush'. And she joked, 'It's the good girls who keep diaries; the bad girls never have the time.'

CONCLUSION

> *Gatsby believed in the green light, the*
> *orgastic future that year by year recedes*
> *before us. It eluded us then, but that's no*
> *matter — tomorrow we will run faster,*
> *stretch out our arms farther... And one*
> *fine morning —*
>
> *So we beat on, boats against the current,*
> *borne back ceaselessly into the past.*

F Scott Fitzgerald, *The Great Gatsby*

The post-war exuberance that fuelled the hedonism of the twenties was, perhaps inevitably, destined to be short-lived. Even as the Bright Young People mixed cocktails in Mayfair, social unrest was growing in Britain, culminating in the General Strike of 1926, when miners, dockers, printers and railwaymen staged a nine-day protest against wages and conditions. At the other end of the social scale, the established society families were losing their lands and fortunes to ever-increasing maintenance bills and taxes.

189

The Wall Street crash of 1929, meanwhile, was about to end the boom years of wealth in the United States and trigger the Great Depression, which would last another ten years.

As the twenties drifted into the thirties, the flappers, dandies and aesthetes of the world moved on with careers, marriages and, in some cases, children, and the endless round of parties gave way to a less frantic existence.

For the Bright Young Things, all across the globe, it was finally time to grow up.

SOURCES AND BIBLIOGRAPHY

Books

Cally Blackman, *Fashion of the Twenties and Thirties* (Heinemann Books)

Barbara Cartland, *We Danced All Night* (Hutchinson)

Jan Dalley, *Diana Mosley* (Faber and Faber)

Frank Dawes, *Not in Front of the Servants* (Hutchinson)

F Scott Fitzgerald, *The Great Gatsby* (Wordsworth Classics)

Jackie Gaff, *20th Century Design: Twenties and Thirties* (Heinemann Books)

Selena Hastings, *Nancy Mitford* (Vintage)

Pamela Horn, *Life Below Stairs in the 20th Century* (Sutton Publishing)

Michael Horsham, *Twenties and Thirties Style* (Grange Books)

The Hutton Getty Picture Library, *The 1920s* (Konemann)

Marie-Jaqueline Lancaster, *Brian Howard: Portrait of a Failure* (Green Candy Press)

Loelia Lindsay, *Grace and Favour: The Memoirs of Loelia, Duchess of Westminster* (Weidenfeld & Nicolson)

Mary S Lovell, *The Mitford Girls* (Abacus)

Kate Meyrick, *Secrets of the 43 Club* (Parkgate Publishing)

Marie Therese Miller-Degenfeld, *Memoirs of Marie Therese Miller-Degenfeld* (Trafford Publishing)

Lucy Moore, *Anything Goes* (Atlantic Books)

Beverley Nichols, *The Sweet and Twenties* (Weidenfeld & Nicolson)

Steve Parker, *20th Century Media: Twenties and Thirties* (Heinemann Books)

Margaret Powell, *Below Stairs* (Pan Books)
Martin Pugh, *We Danced All Night* (Vintage Books)
Peter Sussman (ed.), *Decca: The Letters of Jessica Mitford* (Weidenfeld & Nicolson)
Richard Tames, *Picture History of the 20th Century: The 1920s* (Franklin Watts)
D J Taylor, *Bright Young People* (Vintage Books)
Evelyn Waugh, *Brideshead Revisited* (Penguin)
Evelyn Waugh, *Vile Bodies* (Marshall Cavendish)

Websites

www.1920-30.com
www.aohg.org.uk/twww
www.dailymail.co.uk
www.fotolibra.com
www.havemann.com
www.headoverheelshistory.com
www.independent.co.uk
www.jazzageclub.com

www.jazzbabies.com
www.measuringworth.com
www.nytimes.com
www.proquestk12.com
www.telegraph.co.uk
www.thepeoplehistory.com
www.thetimes.co.uk
www.thisisstafford.co.uk

Page 14: lyrics of 'Tea for Two' written by Irving Caesar.

Pages 20 and 116: 'Bright Young People' and 'The Stately Homes of England' by Noël Coward copyright © NC Aventales AG by permission of Alan Brodie Representation Ltd (www.alanbrodie.com) and Methuen Drama, an imprint of Bloomsbury Publishing Plc.

Page 177: 'Let's Misbehave' (from *Paris*) Words and music by Cole Porter © 1927 (renewed) WB Music Corp. (ASCAP) All Rights Reserved. Used by Permission of Alfred Music Publishing Co., Inc.

Illustrations on pages 130 and 142: Getty Images.

Other illustrations sourced from authentic 1920s matchbook advertising archives, and from the 1920s fashion catalogues of the New York department store B. Altman and Company, and courtesy of Dover Publications, Inc.